"Michael's no jaded pro, his love of the sport is both evident and inspiring—and we are lucky indeed to be privy to his unique insights."
—Davis Phinney, former U.S. professional road cycling champion

"Written in an articulate, fast-flowing style . . . Barry has a keen eye for the minor details of professional life. This is the main reason that the book offers a real and rare sense of what it is like to be a part of a major squad."

—*Cycle Sport*

"What Barry does exceptionally well is write so that pro cyclists and armchair warriors alike can revel in his stories. Barry explains pelotons and defines bike parts so that noncyclists can savor just as many inside jokes as the religious roadie."

—*Boulder Daily Camera*

"Barry provides readers with an inside account of the sublime and mundane aspects of life on the professional racing circuit. A talented writer, Barry explains in terms that even a nonrider is able to understand what team strategies enable Lance to repeatedly win the Tour de France."

—*Staten Island Advance*

INSIDE THE

POSTAL BUS

My Ride with Lance Armstrong and the U.S. Postal Cycling Team

by Michael Barry

Printed in the United States of America.
10 9 8 7 6 5

Distributed in the United States and Canada by Publishers Group West.

Library of Congress Cataloging-in-Publication Data

Barry, Michael, 1975–
    Inside the Postal bus : my ride with Lance Armstrong and the U.S.
       Postal Cycling Team / Michael Barry.
        p. cm.
    ISBN 1-931382-61-1 (pbk. : alk. paper)
          1. U.S. Postal Cycling Team. 2. Bicycle racing. 3. Barry,
          Michael, 1975– I. Title.
    GV1047.U7B37 2005
    796.6'2—dc22

                                  2005004587

VeloPress®
1830 North 55th Street
Boulder, Colorado 80301–2700 USA
303/440-0601 • Fax 303/444-6788 • E-mail velopress@insideinc.com

To purchase additional copies of this book or other VeloPress® books, call 800/234-8356 or visit us at velopress.com.

Cover illustrations © Leo Espinosa
Cover and interior design by Erin Johnson Design
Composition by Kate Hoffhine

TABLE OF CONTENTS

FOREWORD

I first met Michael Barry in Toronto. He had come out to watch a race I was competing in and he was very excited to see the fast action that was about to take place around the Queens Park oval. He was a young lad at that time. He outstretched his hand to shake mine, full of passion for the sport and excited to say hello to a successful professional bike racer.

Now, some decades later, as I leaf through Michael's writings, I find myself filled with the same passion as he had then, wishing I was once again back on the team bus, racing as a professional in the fantastic sport of bike racing.

Of course I miss it and it is so easy to understand why when you read the stories and insights that follow. Yes, surely some things have changed since I retired from competition in 1996. Back then, very few teams sported a team bus, but at present, the team bus is an essential component of the fleet of vehicles that professional squads now depend on. As Michael explains, it is on the bus where the camaraderie of the squad is built and the essence of team spirit is felt. This spirit, common ground, being with the boys—call it what you like—is what I miss the most from my 12-year professional cycling career.

There is no better memory than the feeling of a team working well and one of your mates or yourself winning due to an excellent collective effort. It is fun to be part of a professional group of guys kicking on all cylinders. Some of the characters on my team bus are still in full action: Lance, of course, George Hincapie, Michael (Canadian national team, Atlanta Olympic Games), and so many of the team support crew—from bodyguard Serge to Chef Willy. I still get really fired up to see the guys doing amazing things. I met Lance and some of his teammates when they were training in the Pyrénées for the 2003 Tour de France. We had a nice chat over dinner one evening. I remember Lance saying to me, "Boo [a nickname from my Motorola days], you would have so much fun if you were still racing with us. . . . Man, I am still having fun." The American team initiative that Jim Ochowicz began with 7-Eleven and took to Europe in the 1980s is now a well-oiled, mature group of pros, kicking "bleep" and having fun. Yes, I miss it.

As I read this book I see my experiences in so many of the nuances in Michael's writing. His stories of moving to Europe, getting a place to stay, attending the first team training camp, traveling race to race, drinking cappuccinos, motorpacing, cobblestones. . . . It all comes back and I find myself saying, "Yeah, that's it, Michael. I was there . . . funny." It comes back to me and it's so real and so unique. The life of a professional cyclist on the road is unlike any other professional team athlete and that is what makes the ride so fun. I don't want to candy coat it. It's an extremely hard sport, but I would bet that nine out of 10 guys would do it all again if they could.

It was a privilege to have Michael as my Olympic teammate in Atlanta, Georgia, and it is now a privilege to be asked by Michael to write this foreword.

Read on . . . Michael's stories will put you directly into the realm of a professional cyclist in a very real and yet laid-back manner. The book gives you a great perspective from the inside of the greatest cycling team in this decade. Lance's exploits are well known, but Michael will help you see them from a different angle. You will see how the day-to-day dedication and work ethic of each athlete, the directors, the mechanics, *soigneurs*, bus drivers, and the wives are all part of winning as a team. It's a fun read with interesting insights.

To Michael, thanks for inviting me back on the bus.

To all the boys, continued good luck. . . . Pass the salt!

Steve Bauer

1984 Olympic Games silver medalist
Professional cyclist with La Vie Claire,
7-Eleven, & Motorola

PREFACE

Since Lance Armstrong won the 1999 Tour de France,

virtually every aspiring cyclist has dreamed of riding for the U.S. Postal Service professional cycling team. The team has won the Tour for six consecutive years. U.S. Postal is known throughout the world as Lance Armstrong's team, and Lance is known throughout the world for his incredible and inspiring comeback from testicular cancer. Each year Lance and his teammates have made history by winning big races and showing their strength as a team of great riders who can work together for a common goal.

In the summer of 2004 VeloPress contacted me about writing a book on my experiences on U.S. Postal. I was even presented with a title, *Inside the Postal Bus*, a form of positive feedback from the online rider diaries I had written along that theme for velonews.com.

Everyone knows that these days pro cycling teams have buses to transport the riders as comfortably as possible from hotels to the start of races, from the finish to the next hotel, and from the hotels to the airports. The buses show up at the race start, windows tinted, and the riders step out one by one, climb aboard their bikes, and ride toward the start line. But the spectators rarely, if ever, see the inside of the bus, and they have no idea what goes on behind the tinted windows, what the champions of the sport do before they race to victory.

As a child growing up and being a fan of the sport, I consumed every bit of news about the professional cyclists of the era, not only about their racing but also news about training and every other little bit of insight into who they were and what their lives were like. When I was asked to write this book I thought back to my days as a kid and thought it would be great to convey to spectators what it is like inside the bus of one of the greatest teams in the history of the sport.

I am a cyclist, not a journalist or writer, so the first steps in writing this book were challenging. I didn't know where to start and often-times I wanted to shut down my computer and forget that I had even tried to start writing. But once I found a structure and some persistence, I kept the computer on and the keyboard active, the words built up, and the stories filled the pages.

For me, signing to ride with a world-class professional team like U.S. Postal had been a long time coming. And like the writing of this book, the road to get there had its ups and downs.

ACKNOWLEDGMENTS

Thanks to: DEDE for your love, your persistence, and work ethic. You inspire me. ✷ MOM AND DAD for giving me the opportunities, support, and love that helped me pursue my dreams. Also, thanks for editing, reading, and fueling my ideas as I wrote. ✷ CHRISTIAN AND GEORGE for your help with the book, but most of all for your friendship on and off the bike. You have both taught me a lot about being a bike racer in Europe. ✷ BOB MIONSKE for encouragement, motivation, and the two-hour phone conversations that keep my mind buzzing. ✷ MATT HANSEN for your organization, encouragement, and input. ✷ JANE SOVNDAL for your guidance and edits. ✷ MARGADETTE DEMET for editing and for your kindness. ✷ KEVIN DEMET for your content ideas and insight. ✷ STEVE BAUER for inspiring me as a cyclist and a person. ✷ AMD for providing a computer on which I was able to type the manuscript. ✷ VELOPRESS for giving me the opportunity to write and guiding me through the process. ✷ TAILWIND SPORTS, OAKLEY, PEARL IZUMI, AND ALL OF THE SPONSORS OF THE U.S. POSTAL SERVICE CYCLING TEAM for supporting me in the sport I love. ✷ JOHAN, DIRK, AND LAURENZO for their guidance on the bike, and to all my teammates for their friendship and support. ✷ And LANCE, for inspiring me as a cyclist and a person.

FIRST ENCOUNTERS

*T*he *suitcases came off* the carousel one by one. I fiddled with the change in my pocket, standing behind the rest of the riders as they pulled their bags off. Grabbing mine, I followed Christian Vande Velde's lead toward the exit and the team car. We had just arrived at the Austin, Texas, airport from Denver, with Pavel Padrnos from Prague, Floyd Landis from San Diego, and Antonio Cruz from Los Angeles.

The mild and humid Austin evening air was warm and welcoming compared to Denver's cold December climate. I had left that morning not knowing what to expect in the next week or for the coming 2002 racing season. I shook hands with my new teammates and helped load the bikes and suitcases into two white vans. We took off toward our hotel in Austin, where we would train for a week and get to know each other.

The hotel was in the suburbs of Austin on a golf course—a posh resort with white-gloved valet parking attendants and shiny brass railings. I'd never really been to such a nice place for a training camp. I knew then that riding with the U.S. Postal Service team would be much different from my previous stints with American teams.

I picked up my room key at the front desk. "Peña" was written in black pen beside my name on the key card. Stepping out of the elevator, I followed the arrows to my room. I was still a bit nervous and fumbled with the electronic key. The door opened and Victor Hugo Peña greeted me, wearing only his bikini underwear. He extended his hand and introduced himself.

After settling into my room and chatting with Victor, and learning a little about his home in Colombia and the flight he had endured to Austin, I opened a shopping bag of clothing that lay on the floor beside the bed. Through the white plastic I could see the red, white, and blue of the team uniforms. Pulling out the jersey, I placed it on the bed, along with the shorts, jacket, socks, and tights. I had seen the jerseys on television, in pictures, and at a handful of North American events, but I had never put one on. I folded the clothing up and laid it in my suitcase, ready for the following day's training.

Victor began to pull on a team sweatsuit, covering up his underwear and his shark tattoo. I had heard that his nickname was *Tiburon*, or "the Shark," for his prowess in the pool prior to his career as a cyclist.

He looked at me and said, "Hey *mang*, we can go for dinner now."

We made our way downstairs to a room that had been set aside especially for the team. Four round tables were set, with some of the seats already taken. I walked around the room and introduced myself to everybody. I had spoken only with Johan Bruyneel, the team director, on the phone and had met very few of the other staff members before. I sat with two Americans, Christian and George Hincapie, where I was somewhat comfortable.

Halfway through the meal, Lance Armstrong walked into the room. He was wearing a wool-lined denim jacket, jeans, and a baseball cap. Making the rounds to each table, he introduced himself, stopping to talk with each rider briefly. He got to our table and came over to me.

"Hi Michael," he said. "I'm Lance."

Lance sat and talked for awhile with George and Christian about the off-season, his newborn twin daughters, what he had been up to in the past months, and his Christmas plans. I couldn't stop thinking about what this guy had accomplished on the bike. It was just so hard to believe, looking at him, a normal-looking guy, that he could go that fast on a bicycle. I watched and listened to the conversation, still too nervous and apprehensive to say much. For the last 19 years, since I was five, I had wanted to race with a professional European-based team. And here I was—that day was finally here.

In the early mornings in Austin we lifted weights in the gym, building core muscles that don't get used much during the season. We spent the rest of the morning riding for a couple of hours in the hills around the area. The rides were fairly fast; we sprinted for town signs and raced each other up sections of gravel road. Lance knew the roads well since Austin is his hometown, and he acted as our guide for the week. He also took us out on the town, to his favorite restaurants and hangouts. By the end of the week, the new guys felt like members of the team and had begun to find their places. Johan oversaw the whole operation with Lance's input.

"What do you think of the team—are you enjoying yourself here?" Johan asked me at a relaxed team dinner one night, a glass of wine in one hand, a small quiche in the other.

"I do like it. It was not what I expected," I answered. "I like how relaxed it is. The guys seem cool."

"Good," he answered. He asked me the same question several times again throughout the week, checking to make sure I was okay.

Victor and I talked for hours before bed each night, turning the light off well after midnight. He would tell me about training in Tucson with Lance, learning English by listening to all the guys on the team, the party that followed Lance's third Tour victory in 2001, and his home in Colombia. In Austin, Victor went shopping every day, filling our room with an inflatable chair, which he intended to take home and give to his brother, as well as pairs of Nike shoes, T-shirts, and more.

Back in the spring of 1996, I had boarded a plane in my hometown of Toronto that would take me to Geneva, Switzerland. The overseas flight was seven hours, and the entire time I was buzzing with thoughts and emotions while my CD player was spinning out electronic music that matched my excitement about the future. On the flight, I let my emotions flow out onto paper as I drew and wrote on my notepad.

As we neared the airport in Geneva, the woman beside me turned to look at me and said, "You're a motivated student. You must have gotten a lot of work done on the flight." I explained to her that, no, I hadn't been working but that I had a lot going through my head since

I had just chosen a new path in my life. I told her that I had actually quit university to pursue my dream of being a professional cyclist in Europe.

"Oh," she responded, dryly. "Well, good luck."

I had stepped on the plane thinking that I would either be back in Canada living at my parents' house and going back to school in two weeks, or I would be staying in France for the entire season. I ended up remaining in France for the year, coming back to Canada only for the national championships and to the United States for the Olympics in Atlanta.

The town of Annemasse, France, sponsored a small amateur racing team. Looking to increase public interest in the team—and also to bolster its roster with foreigners—the team had contacted the Canadian national team coach in search of riders, and that's how I ended up finding a home in Annemasse, a suburb of Geneva across the Swiss-French border in the heart of the French Alps. I felt alive in France; mountains and ideal roads for cycling surrounded the town. Every road I took on my bicycle led to a new adventure. I had begun to live my dream, racing as an amateur on the roads on which the legends of the Tour had battled for the yellow jersey.

A woman named Gabrielle Cheneval owned my apartment, and her family soon became my adopted French family. They made sure I was well fed and taken care of. The Chenevals taught me about French culture, how to choose a good baguette, and how to select mushrooms in the woods. The team supported me with everything I needed to be a bike racer, and Christian Rumeau, the team director, advised me on tactics, diet, and how to live as a bike racer. Christian had been director to one of the greatest riders in the history of the sport, 1980s cycling icon Sean Kelly, for most of his career and had guided many cycling professionals through their great years.

For two and a half years, I lived in Annemasse and raced in Europe with the Annemasse team and, on occasion, with the Canadian national team. These years shaped me as a cyclist and I would have most likely moved on to a professional team in Europe if I hadn't endured two bad crashes in one season.

The first crash occurred in the Alps. I came flying down a descent in the rain, slid out on a corner, and crashed on sharp rocks. The impact broke my femur and the rocks tore open my skin. To recover, I returned home to Canada, and then went to Colorado to train in the mountains and regain some fitness before returning to France. The second crash happened just after I had come back and was racing in the Tour of Toledo in Spain. Again, on a descent, I veered off the road, flew over the handlebars, and landed in a ditch face-first. Immediately my back hurt. I was given a new bike, and I climbed on and pedaled away, only to stop and get into the team car a few kilometers later.

My season was over, and I spent three months in an orthopedic corset, my upper body immobilized. During my recovery, I wasn't able to ride my bike, and I didn't really know if I would race again. I returned to Canada to be with my parents and heal.

I tried to keep my morale up by walking in Toronto and doing projects around the house. Soon the three months had passed and I was out of the corset, riding a home trainer, and swimming at the local pool. The Canadian winter blew in, and I decided to return to Boulder, Colorado, where I had trained earlier in the year, to rebuild my fitness and visit a girl I had met, Dede Demet, an American professional cyclist racing with the Saturn team. A mutual friend and cyclist, Clara Hughes, who was also training in Boulder at the time, had introduced us. After a few weeks of training together in Colorado's Front Range, we were falling in love. When I returned home to Canada, we spoke daily on the phone. She motivated me to work on getting back my fitness, giving me confidence when I thought I would never be able to reach a strong competitive level again.

In the spring of 1998, I was back racing in France with the Annemasse team, winning races but not feeling quite as content. I missed Dede. I moved back to Canada and was offered a position with the U.S.–based Saturn cycling team. I accepted, returned to Boulder with Dede, and we were married in the autumn of 1998.

I raced with Saturn for two more seasons, in 1999 and 2000. But in 2001 I felt a need for a change in my career. I decided I would either race in Europe with a professional team or stop racing to go back to school and pursue other goals. By the season's end, I had a contract with U.S. Postal, the premier team in the world, whose leader was one of sport's greatest champions.

In 1980 I began pedaling my bike up and down Petman Avenue and past my house in Toronto, Ontario. As a child, as soon as I could open a book and turn the pages, I was immersed in the volumes of cycling books and magazines my dad had on his shelves. My heroes were the legends of the Tour de France, the classics, and the world championships: Eddy Merckx, Laurent Fignon, and Steve Bauer. When I raced my friends around the block I was "Eddy the Cannibal," the hills were the Pyrénées, and my parents' cobbled drive was the fabled Arenberg Forest. The girl next door, Jennifer, was our *soigneur* (the caretaker or massage therapist who works with cyclists), handing out bags of candy to us while we sped around the block.

As a youngster I remember quickly hiding the big volume of cycling history I was reading, switching off the overhead light and feigning sleep before the door opened and my sitter, Auna, a 16-year-old girl I secretly had a crush on despite the 10-year age difference, popped her head in to make sure I was indeed asleep. She guessed pretty quickly that I was awake, since the big blue book was peeking out from under my pillow. As I peered out at her from a half-open eyelid, she glanced at her watch and told me to get to sleep, that it was well past 11 p.m. She would take the book with her downstairs, glancing at the title briefly and shaking her head. In Canada few people rode bicycles and even fewer owned libraries of books on cycling.

At six, I devoured everything I could about the sport, my teachers reporting to my parents that they saw bike wheels turning in my eyes as they tried to teach me math or science. I would go to sleep with images from the magazines rolling through my mind: Merckx on Mont Ventoux, Luis Ocaña crashing in the yellow jersey, Roger de Vlaeminck navigating the cobblestone roads in the French cycling classic, Paris-Roubaix.

As a professional today, my passion for the sport hasn't changed, but I have made my childhood dreams a reality. I am racing in the Pyrénées and over the cobbles of northern Europe and it is a lot more painful than I ever imagined it would be. As children we set goals for ourselves and believe they will one day come true. Many kids have played in the garden dreaming of going to space or playing hockey in the NHL, but once adolescence hits and the pressures of parents, friends, and society, they are usually forced to pursue another path. We are told to stop dreaming and face reality. I am fortunate that I was given opportunities to follow my dream, with the guidance and support of my parents, my wife, my school, and my friends. The dream has moments when it can begin to fade, but when I am out on my bike, feeling the pedals beneath my feet, flying up a climb or down a mountain, the dream remains vital and I appreciate that I am living it every day.

Every rider on U.S. Postal has questioned the path he has taken in the sport at one point or another. Most of us have crashed heavily, been

NO TRAINING WHEELS: *The author began racing on a Mariposa bike that his father built.*

injured, and wondered whether we would ride a bike again. Succeeding as a cyclist requires patience, persistence, and talent. Even Lance, one of the most accomplished cyclists to race a bicycle, and one of the most talented athletes ever to live, still questions whether he can win, or whether he can get in shape in time, and shows humility and respect to the other riders and the sport.

Racing in Europe as professionals is particularly challenging for the non-European riders. From a young age we travel overseas for the cycling season and go home to visit our families only in the autumn. We often live in rough housing on our own or in lonely hotels. Survival is tough and many riders decide to head back home to school rather than to persist. The Australians, New Zealanders, and the American cyclists who do stick with it are successful because of their mental strength—in the European ranks the foreign riders are often known for being the toughest. The United States and Australia have few cyclists at the amateur level who turn professional, yet both are among the most successful nations in the pro peloton because of their tenacity.

Today the U.S. Postal team travels the world to race before massive audiences in the most famous races in the sport. But at the end of the day, when we're all kicking back and relaxing in a hotel lobby over tea or coffee, we are all still just a bunch of kids pedaling bikes, happily giving every ounce of energy we have to our sport.

Cycling has an incredible history—a history rich in pain, triumph, struggle, and inspiration. It is a sport that made me dream as a kid, kept me out until after dark in the streets with my mom worried sick, taught me how to persist and be victorious and how to lose and keep trying, showed me the world, introduced me to my best friends and my wife, and keeps me living my dream as an adult.

Cyclists don't question pushing through incredible pain. When we fall off our bikes, our thoughts immediately turn from the crash toward making it to the finish. We don't think about the burn of the cuts or the pain in our bones, but instead focus on making it to the finish line so that we can be at the start line the next day. We only discover the physical damage done to our bodies when we get to the hotel and the team doctors look us over. Or sometimes the pain is simply too intense to continue and we are forced to abandon and get in the ambulance.

Retiring from a race leaves a pit in my stomach. I feel empty, because I have not been able to complete a goal with the team. The biggest challenge is waking up the morning after, hearing the guys talk about the race, seeing them pack their bags, pin on their numbers, and climb aboard the bus.

As my U.S. Postal teammate, fellow Canadian and mountain bike ace Ryder Hesjedal said, "I look forward to long transfers on the bus. It's wicked."

"Why?" George Hincapie asked.

"Because it's relaxing. We can kick back, legs up, and take it easy before the race. There are pastries, drinks, leather recliners, and an espresso machine. The bus rocks."

In the bus, the team prepares for the event and relaxes before the race, without distraction. In the bus we are the team, together.

CHAPTER TWO

A FRESH START

It was a typical day at training camp. At 6:30 in the morning I woke up and headed for the bathroom. The aroma of coffee hung heavily in the stale bedroom air. The bathroom door was slightly ajar, and a shaft of light penetrated the darkness of the room. I pushed open the door, squinting at the light. Roberto Heras, the winner of the 2000 Vuelta a España, was sitting on the closed toilet seat in his pajamas, a book in one hand and a mug of strong black coffee in the other.

Roberto looked up at me and said, "Hey, man, you need the bathroom? I can't sleep. I made coffee. You want coffee?"

Having just traveled from Europe to arrive at the team training camp in Solvang, California, my roommate Roberto was being considerate. Although he was feeling jet-lagged, he didn't want to wake me.

The first training camp the U.S. Postal team attends is in December in Lance's hometown of Austin, Texas. The camp is held to acquaint the new riders with the team. A select group of American riders on the team's upcoming roster—those who did not race frequently during the last months of the season—are asked to attend. The atmosphere is casual and relaxed, training sessions are loosely structured, and we stay in a swank hotel.

At the end of January, the entire team is flown to California. At the Solvang camp, we train consistently every day and focus on getting fit for the racing season. After the Solvang camp we fly to Scottsdale, an easily accessible city with predictable weather, where we meet with our sponsors for a weekend before flying to Europe to begin the racing season.

Solvang is an unusual little Danish-themed town just north of Santa Barbara. With its rolling hills, mountains, and long valleys, the countryside around Solvang is ideal for training. There are few cars on the roads—mainly agricultural vehicles tending to the local vineyards, vegetable fields, or horse pastures. Many of the premier equestrian team stables in the United States are around Solvang, and several of our training loops take us by the home of Secretariat, one of the most successful racehorses in American history. On days when the group is feeling adventurous, we ride the dirt roads into the hills and toward the coast. On easier days, we roll by the vineyards and alongside the freshly tilled fields.

It's become an annual tradition for the team to assemble in Solvang to begin training for the year. The non-Americans get a little taste of American culture, and the North Americans get to spend a few extra weeks close to home before heading overseas for the season. The team was comprised of 25 riders during the 2004 season, with half of it made up of North American riders: Lance, George Hincapie (the only rider to have ridden alongside Lance during each of his six Tour de France victories), and Floyd Landis were the three Americans that raced the 2004 Tour. The others, Dave Zabriskie, Damon Kluck, Patrick McCarty, Mike Creed, Antonio Cruz, Robbie Ventura, and Kenny Labbe raced with the team both in North America and in Europe. The roster was completed with Europeans and South Americans. José Luis "Chechu" Rubiera, Manuel "Triki" Beltran, José Azevedo, Benjamin Noval, Viatcheslav "Eki" Ekimov, and Pavel Padrnos filled out the nine-man Tour team in 2004, while Victor Hugo Peña, Daniel Rincon, Benoit Joachim, Guennadi Mikhailov, Jurgen Van den Broeck, Stijn Devolder, and Max Van Heeswijk strengthened the team for the other races throughout the season. Canadian Ryder Hesjedal raced with the team on occasion throughout the spring of 2004 prior to returning to mountain bike racing, his true discipline for the Olympics in Athens. The youngest riders on the team were only 21, while "Eki," the oldest, was 38.

Because the team races 150 days of the year, 25 riders are needed to accommodate the schedule. At three-week stage races, or grand tours—of which there are three during the year, the Giro d'Italia in May, the Tour de France in July, and the Vuelta a España in September— nine-man teams are required. The other races on the calendar require the team to have anywhere from six to eight riders, depending on the event. The race organizers decide on the size of the field of racers, or peloton, they can accommodate in the race, as they must feed and house the riders, while cycling's governing body, the Union Cycliste Internationale (UCI) puts limitations on the size of the peloton to keep the racing safe and interesting.

At the annual Solvang camp, we really get to know our new team-mates—the guys with whom we will spend weeks on the road, sharing hotel rooms and endless hours of riding and racing. The camp is not just an intense period of training; it is a time for us to get fitted on our new bikes, get sized and fitted in our new team clothing, and for the team to be officially announced to the press. It's a very busy time. From our shorts to our bikes, everything needs to be sized and built up. Each day prior to our rides, we arrive early to perfect our positions on our new bikes, down to the millimeter.

The training rides are the focal point of our days. In 2004 the team split into two groups, a slow and a fast group, because one big group is simply too large for training. You spend too much time drafting each other's wheels and not enough time pedaling against the wind. The fast group can work on conditioning for the upcoming classics, the historic and prestigious early-season races in northern Europe. The classics are the toughest single-day races on the calendar. The riders race in the cold spring months of March and April for six hours or more over cobbled Roman roads in front of hundreds of thousands of spectators and millions more who are watching on television. The spring classics all take place in Belgium, the Netherlands, and France, intermittently through the week and on the weekends.

The slower group at training camp focuses on the Tour de France and events later in the year. The younger, less mature riders on the team are also put with the slower group so that they have a chance to progress without too much physical or mental stress. It is important for the rookies to ease into the sport as it is easy to burn out a young motivated rider with too many race days, too many hours of training, and too much mental stress.

GRAHAM WATSON

ROLLING: *Training camp is one of the few times the team is all together for a ride.*

At the training camps we ride two-by-two, like a team of horses, with each pair taking a five-minute turn on the front in the wind before retiring to the draft at the back of the group to recover. We ride this way so that the pace stays even. Everybody works hard on the front at steady intervals, and we are tight against the shoulder of the road so that cars can pass.

When somebody has a mechanical problem we all slow down. Then when that person is back in the group, someone will yell, "Everybody is here," and the riders at the front will get back up to speed.

While climbing in the middle of the bunch, Lance will often say, "Everybody's here" in jest, insinuating the riders on the front aren't going fast enough. It is a little mind game that makes everybody chuckle while we pedal away for six hours.

The team rides in 2004 were harder than they were my first two years on the team. The fast group often ended up racing over the hills and sprinting for town signs. Our Spanish rider Chechu Rubiera joked that we should have been pinning numbers on for our training rides since everyone was so motivated to race each other. I guess we're born competitive.

At the Solvang camp we are given almost everything we need for the season—for both casual wear and race clothing—to keep us comfortable in the cold Belgian spring as well as the hot Spanish summer. We also have race clothing designed for extreme weather conditions, such as light jerseys that are well ventilated for summer heat and thick jerseys and shorts for cold winter days. There is always a palpable excitement among the team when receiving our bags and bags of clothing. And even though most of the riders on the team are still excited when they get a new piece of team clothing, by the end of the season it's hard to pull any of it on anymore because we've been wearing it for half of the year and are sick of it.

Along with the rider roster, the new team jerseys are often unveiled to the media at the Solvang training camp. I think most of the team was pleased with the new uniform and the changes that were made for the 2004 season. The jerseys showed up well in the peloton and could be identified from a distance. There were a few new sponsors on the jerseys: AMD, a computer processor company, was featured prominently on the jersey and shorts; Outdoor Life Network, a sponsor that followed Lance and the team for the entire season, documenting our team's progress on cable television; Bissell, a vacuum cleaner company that joined the team halfway through 2003, featured prominently on the back of the jersey.

When we first show up at camp and have a different team of riders around us at dinner or on the rides, it can feel a bit surreal, especially when you see that a rider who was part of the competition the previous year will now be wearing the same U.S. Postal team suit as your own.

Once everyone has been given their new clothing, the team really begins to take shape. We all look the same at dinner, on the bike, and while we stroll through town. The staff puts together the press kits, complete with team photos and postcards for the season. In the photos we all look tired from training and the Europeans look extra tired from jet lag.

At the 2004 Solvang camp we had a few other additions at the team meals. Our most notable new dinner guest was musician and pop icon Sheryl Crow, who Lance had met and had begun dating during the off-season. It was a change for the team, but after a few days at the camp we became comfortable in her presence. She went on some of our rides, fully equipped and nicely positioned on her new Trek bike. Despite having to eat with a bunch of cyclists who were talking about racing most of the time, she seemed to enjoy the atmosphere and quickly caught on to what the sport was about.

In Solvang we are free to spend the afternoons doing what we want: we can kick back and chat, nap and eat, do a little shopping or reading. Ah, the life of a bike racer. Some days we go to the movies or to the grocery store for snacks. Whenever there is a bit of downtime, the Europeans are often at electronic superstores buying mp3 players, cameras, and computer stuff.

During the last week of training camp, the workload increases and the competitive spirit within the team becomes more subdued, as everybody gets a little tired. Throughout the final week, we ride our bikes between four and six hours each day.

In 2004 we left Solvang for a weekend in Scottsdale, Arizona, for our sponsor camp. The two days consisted of fine meals and a room in a nice hotel. We met and rode with our sponsors and friends of the team, many of whom are avid cyclists themselves. The rides in Scottsdale were police escorted, which is always nice, especially since Scottsdale and Phoenix are quite congested. We were allowed to blow through stoplights and signs and take up most of the road, generally making quite a scene. It can be exhilarating to pass irate drivers who would normally blast their horn, while overtaking us and giving us the bird out the window, yelling for us to get off the road.

At the Austin training camp in 2002, a behemoth of a pickup truck overtook us, horn blaring, and then as soon as he pulled in front of the team, the driver slammed on his brakes. Reacting to his aggression, Lance yelled and some of the riders threw their bottles at the truck. The truck driver stuck his head out the window, looking back at the group, and shouted, "Get off the road you bunch of f—ing pussies." Lance approached the driver's window, and suddenly the driver realized just who he was yelling at. He sheepishly said, "Sorry, Lance," rolled up his window, and sped away.

The 2004 sponsor weekend nicely capped off the two weeks we had been training together. Good food, a few glasses of wine, and some good laughs left everybody in high spirits for the upcoming year. Movie star Robin Williams is a great fan of Lance and our team, as well as a keen cyclist. After a training ride, Robin, still wearing his cycling gear with his helmet strapped tight on his head, did a stand-up comedy routine for over an hour at a barbecue lunch. The Spanish guys had no clue what he was saying, but his gestures and imitations were entertaining enough to keep them huddled around the bonfire. The weekend was the one chance we got to spend some quality time with the people who support us all year.

The team roster grew by a few riders in the 2004 season. We needed the new additions since in 2003 illness and injury often left us at the start line with fewer riders than other teams. Starting a difficult stage race with six riders instead of eight is a bad way to begin a race. Johan and Dirk Demol (the team's assistant director) often had to call the race organizers to tell them we could not field a full team at an event, as there were simply not enough riders within the team to fill the roster due to illness or injury.

Every year a few riders from the team leave to join other teams or to retire. Certain characters are really missed and their absence is noticeable. But there are also a few new guys who fit into the team immediately and easily hang out with the team veterans. Generally everybody fits together well; there aren't really any cliques.

The new team riders added for the 2004 season were great additions. There were many young guys within the new group, many Americans, and their enthusiasm was good to see. The new Spanish-speaking additions counted on the vets, like Victor and Chechu, to tell them what was going on and how things worked.

Chechu is the most educated rider on the team. In the spring of 2004, he graduated from university with an engineering degree, an

impressive accomplishment as there are few professional cyclists who
have any education beyond high school. Chechu was my roommate the
first time I rode the Vuelta a España, in 2002. He would pack textbooks
to read during the bus ride to the stage start and spend the night after
the stages with a textbook on his lap, pen in one hand, figuring out
wiring patterns on different machines. Not only did his intellect impress
me, but also his work ethic and moti-
vation to complete his schooling.

*ROBERTO IS ONE OF
BEST CLIMBERS IN
THE WORLD, WHICH IS WHY
U.S. POSTAL HIRED HIM,
AND HE WAS OFTEN PIVOTAL
IN HELPING LANCE DEFEAT
HIS ADVERSARIES IN THE
HIGH MOUNTAINS.*

During the 2003 training camp, I
roomed with Roberto Heras, and in
2004 I was paired with José
Azevedo. After winning his second
Tour of Spain (Vuelta a España) in
September 2003, Roberto was
offered a lucrative contract with a
Spanish team, Liberty Seguros. He
opted to take that offer because as the Liberty team leader he would have
opportunities to win the Tour de France himself. Roberto is one of the best
climbers in the world, which is why U.S. Postal hired him, and he was
often pivotal in helping Lance defeat his adversaries in the high mountains. On the team he felt confined because his job was to help Lance at
the Tour rather than racing for himself. On the U.S. Postal team there isn't
enough room for two leaders at the Tour; Lance had proven himself as the
clear leader so Roberto was forced to work for the team. As a Spaniard,
Roberto would also be in a familiar atmosphere at Liberty Seguros.

Roberto's departure left a vacant spot we needed to fill. The team
went looking for a replacement and found José Azevedo, or "the Ace,"
as Lance has affectionately and appropriately nicknamed him. The

MISSION ACCOMPLISHED: *Johan Bruyneel, Roberto Heras, and Dirk Demol celebrating Heras's Vuelta victory in 2003.*

cycling press said Roberto's shoes would be hard to fill, and José, a quiet Portuguese rider, never said a word—he just let his legs prove his worth throughout the season.

With ONCE, a Spanish team sponsored by a national lottery, José had been Joseba Beloki's right-hand man and great friend for several years, and achieved many great results himself. After ONCE folded, he signed with MAIA, a Portuguese team, before being contacted by our team. MAIA released José from his contractual obligations and gave him the freedom to pursue his goals and career with U.S. Postal.

At the 2004 Critérium International, an early-season stage race in northern France, our team gathered at the podium near the start line and the promoters announced the notable achievements of each rider. When José was called up, they listed off top 10 overall placings in the Tour de France and the Giro d'Italia (Tour of Italy).

Impressed by his results, Lance looked over at him and said, "Damn, that's pretty good, man." José is a champion, but he is also an understated, kind guy. He's known as one of the best workers in cycling, and his efforts on behalf of his teammates are memorable to all the riders in the peloton, often overshadowing his own sterling achievements.

When European riders arrive on the team, they are expected to speak or learn English, the most common language among riders and staff. On the race radios, which we all wear during the race and use to communicate with our team, we speak primarily English. From team meetings to e-mails, nearly all of the communications are carried out in English.

When we are at camp or at races, Johan tries to pair a foreigner with a native English-speaking rider, or he puts a team veteran in a room with a new rider on the squad. Johan is fluent in several languages and will translate for the foreign riders when necessary.

The one problem with the Spanish riders and others learning English from the other riders is that they tend to pick up swear words and slang, just as I tend to know certain foul expressions in Spanish, Dutch, Italian, and German. Bike-racing English is what we speak and bike-racing language is what they learn, which can lead to amusing moments when the words are unknowingly used and abused in everyday conversation. The hip-hop played on the stereo in the team bus is most likely another obstacle to learning proper English.

At the 2004 training camp, José wanted to speak in English and learn more, and I wanted to improve my Spanish since I spend most of the year in Spain racing and training. So he talked to me in English and I would talk in Spanish, with the English-Spanish dictionary often open nearby.

When Victor Hugo Peña came to the team, he didn't speak a word of English. He tells stories about training with Lance for six hours and not being able to say a word. Early on in his time with U.S. Postal, Victor couldn't understand why the milk tasted so strange, so rich. One morning, Lance went to fix himself a cup of coffee but the half and half was gone. He questioned Victor, who answered that he had just had a big glass and finished off the carton. Lance reportedly cleared it up in his characteristically succinct way, "Victor, it's for the f—ing coffee."

While Victor and Lance were training in Tucson, a barking and vicious dog ran toward their group. Lance was deep in conversation with a friend and unaware of the dog. Victor wanted to alert Lance to the danger but couldn't; he didn't know the word for "dog" in English. He searched for the word as he shouted to Lance, and Lance responded with, "What?" By the time Victor finally made Lance aware of the dog, it was already in their path. They swerved and missed the dog. Vic realized it was critical that he learn more English as quickly as possible.

Now Victor speaks English well and can communicate just fine with the team and in conversation. Daniel Rincon, a new Colombian recruit for the 2004 season, doesn't speak a word of English and has asked Victor to listen carefully at meetings so he can translate for him afterward.

Daniel's brother, Olivero Rincon, was a legend of the pro peloton in the late-1980s and 1990s. Olivero won many big races and was an ace climber who consistently finished in the top 10 at the Vuelta a España and select Tour de France mountain stages. Daniel is quiet and always has a smile on his face, even when suffering in a strung-out peloton.

Following the 2004 Tour of Murcia in southern Spain, I drove back to my Spanish home in Girona with Daniel. It was a long trip, so I asked him to split the driving with me. He hesitated at first, but he eventually took the wheel. I sensed he was nervous and I began to regret my decision to have him drive. He looked at me and asked about the gears. He had never driven an automatic. I put the car in drive and said, "Go." The car took off like a bullet and then slowed to a snail's pace. When we got to the highway, he stopped just as we were going to merge. I yelled at him to go again and he hit the accelerator.

We got rolling and he began to feel more comfortable in the car. Turning to me, he said, "Are you nervous with my driving?"

I shrugged, trying not to hurt his feelings, even though I thought he was awfully sketchy behind the wheel. He told me it was his first time driving on a highway since there are only two-lane roads where he lives in Colombia. Once he became comfortable with the torque on the accelerator and the sensitivity of the brakes, he was not bad, and we made it home okay.

At training camp José quickly found out that I appreciate a good cup of coffee, since we made it in our room each morning before heading down to breakfast. He told me that Portugal is known for its good espresso and that you can find high-quality coffee all over the country. When we arrived at the Volta ao Algarve in Portugal, he brought me some of his favorite coffee beans to sample. Every race since then, he brings me different roasts from home to try.

Butter is never placed on Spanish dinner tables, but olive oil is. The olive oil is often excellent, fruity, and seldom rancid. Much of the Spanish olive production is used in Italian olive oil. Spain exports the olives to Italy, where they are pressed and poured into Italian-labeled bottles and sold throughout the world.

Triki Beltran comes from the south of Spain. He grew up the son of an olive farmer close to the town of Jaen in Andalusia. Triki is extremely passionate about olives and olive oil. In his passport his name reads Manuel Beltran, but he earned the nickname "Triki" because of his weakness for cookies. El Triki is the Spanish version of "Cookie Monster" on Sesame Street. Few people call him Manuel, and in 2004 his leader's jersey at the Vuelta a España had *El Triki* printed on it. Despite the fact that Triki consumes more cookies and olive oil than the rest of us, he is by far the skinniest rider on the team.

After racing in Andalusia, I began to understand why Triki obsesses over olives. Millions of olive trees line the roads as far as the eye can see. We raced for hun-

DESPITE THE FACT THAT TRIKI CONSUMES MORE COOKIES AND OLIVE OIL THAN THE REST OF US, HE IS BY FAR THE SKINNIEST RIDER ON THE TEAM.

dreds of kilometers and saw nothing but olive trees. The air had a pungent odor, and the roads were stained with the oil of this small fruit. Each fall after the racing season is finished, Triki heads back to the fields and helps out his father with the olive harvest and the pressing.

Triki brings his father's olive oil to each race for us to use with our pasta or rice at meals. Often he'll look around the table to make sure everybody is using his oil and not the restaurant's. Whenever a new rider comes to the team or a guest sits at the table, Triki starts in, seizing any opportunity to promote his product. He focuses so intensely on teaching us about olives that he doesn't notice George Hincapie mocking him with imitations of Forrest Gump's friend Bubba talking about shrimp. Triki is a Spanish Bubba, a true salesman for his business.

Triki struggles with English more than anyone on the team. In the south of Spain, the Andalusians speak with a distinctive accent, typically dropping the "s" in words. When they cheer for Lance, they say, "Armtrong!" It is said that Andalusians slur their words during the hot summer months because they don't have enough energy to enunciate properly.

Even some of the other Spanish riders on the team have a hard time understanding Triki's Spanish. At the 2004 Pays Basque, a tough stage race in the Basque region of Spain, we faced snow at the start. Triki pointed outside and said, "Look, no." Upset with all the laughter when he spoke in English, he then said, "Triki no peak Engli, Triki only peak pani."

Triki has improved his English a lot since joining the team in 2003 and understands much of what we talk about at our meetings. I can understand his difficulty in learning English, as the mouth and tongue move entirely differently when speaking Spanish. Racing frequently with Spanish-speaking riders has been good for my Spanish. I speak "cycling Spanish," the majority of which I have picked up either at the dinner table or while watching bike races on Spanish television.

The riders' habits often reveal interesting insights into their cultural differences. The Spanish guys on the team wear pajamas whenever they get a chance. As soon as they get back to the hotel room after riding, racing, breakfast, lunch, or dinner, they slip into their PJs. They love pajamas printed with little bears or other animals. José has a wicked pair of blue PJs with white ghosts all over them.

It often feels like in our male-dominated subculture, we are part of a fraternity at the races. The jokes and crude language flow. Men make up the majority of the team staff and women rarely compete at the same events. Dede was at the Tour of Flanders in the spring of 2004, and she stayed at the same hotel as our team. I think some of the guys, cooped up in a Belgian hotel room for weeks without their wives or girlfriends, enjoyed seeing her T-Mobile teammates at dinner in the evening. Our team was on their best behavior, but Pavel Padrnos was a little flustered when my wife came to his door to visit his roommate Antonio Cruz, a friend of Dede's whom she had raced with since she was a teenager. Thinking it was Tony at the door, Pavel answered it with nothing on. He quickly told her to wait and closed the door. Dede could hear him fumbling around the room, finding his sweats. We all laughed about it, but I think perhaps Pavel remained embarrassed, because the next few times he saw Dede he turned red.

The next time Dede saw Pavel was at the end of the season in San Francisco, and Pavel, after kissing her on the cheek in Euro fashion, shyly said, "I wore some clothing this time."

Our team members are expected to be professional and to arrive at the races in good shape. What we eat or do to get fit is our business. This big difference comes from the European and American mentalities about the sport. Cycling in Europe is so steeped in lore, tradition, and history that often riders or teams will do things out of long-standing tradition—for example, maybe they do some rituals only because Italian icon and champion cyclist Fausto Coppi did it that way in the 1940s, not because it makes sense.

José came from the Spanish team ONCE, which operated quite differently than U.S. Postal. Manolo Saiz, the former ONCE team director, guides and closely controls his riders. He watches them at dinner and gives them strict training programs to follow. Manolo insists that all his riders wear tights and long jerseys no matter what the temperature. This goes back to the days when people believed that if you got chilled you would get sick, so you should keep your limbs covered to keep your muscles warm. Nobody seemed to worry about dehydration or heat exhaustion.

Johan graduated from Manolo's school. He rode for much of his career and achieved top results under Manolo's guidance. I think Johan has taken the good from Manolo and left behind some of the old-school ideas. He doesn't bug us about our diets, but he runs the team like a well-oiled machine. Johan, much like Manolo, controls the team from the top down. He oversees everything from travel to the training programs to the bikes and gear choices for the races. Both Manolo and Johan like to know everything going on in the team, so they can handle volatile situations before they erupt and recognize when things are going well.

Both Johan Bruyneel and Dirk Demol are Belgian and are accomplished riders. Johan was a stage racer and a climber with sterling results in the Vuelta, the Tour (even holding the yellow jersey), and many shorter stage races. Dirk was the antithesis, a classics rider who was at home on the cobbled climbs in Flanders or the cobbled Roman roads in northern France. Today, they direct the team on the terrain where they felt most comfortable as riders. Johan follows in the first team car at the Tour de France, calling out tactics as the team climbs the Alps, while Dirk drives the first team car during Paris-Roubaix, a race he won in 1988.

Our former teammate, Christian Vande Velde, rode for Manolo's new team, Liberty Seguros, during the 2004 season alongside Roberto Heras. Christian went through the same culture shock José experienced when he came over to U.S. Postal. Christian was amazed at the amount of riding they do at their camps, how their diet is closely monitored, how they are pinched to see whether they have gained weight, and also how all the riders on the team are very close and do everything together, whether training for six hours or going for a coffee at night.

Another personality the team missed in 2004 was Matt White, an Australian. "Whitey" and I spent many days and nights rooming together in 2003—so many, in fact, that Dede counted them and figured I had spent more days in the same room with Whitey than I had with her.

The most upbeat guy on the team, Whitey was a true teammate. Not only would he give everything he had for the leader, but he would also keep everybody's morale up when things turned grim. We got along well and attributed it to our Commonwealth ties; we both have a mellow attitude and a Brit sense of humor.

During the 2003 Vuelta, I roomed with Whitey from start to finish. Early on his wife, Jane, told me that Matt was notorious for not putting the caps back on bottles and tubes properly. She was right. Every second day Whitey had something leaking in his bag. Shampoo wasn't too bad, but his gear was soon showing traces of the chocolate-flavored energy gel and curry sauce he was carrying around Spain—not a pretty sight.

Whitey used the curry sauce for the potatoes our Chef Willy cooks up for us after each stage. I don't think Willy was a big fan of Whitey's curry sauce, but the idea behind the potatoes is that they are high in carbohydrates, easy to digest, satisfying, and full of potassium and vitamins. With Triki's olive oil and a bit of salt, they are very tasty and satisfying.

Whitey has a cast-iron stomach and on many occasions he has impressed me with what he can put down and digest. On occasion things go a bit wrong and he ends up on the toilet for a few days, but for the most part he

BON APPÉTIT: *Chef Willy Balmat serves up a dish to Manuel Beltran.*

is okay. Let him within 10 feet of a seafood buffet and it can get messy.

At the bottom of a mountain just outside of Barcelona, Whitey combined pizza with *horchata*, a sweet Mexican drink of rice milk and cinnamon, during a 40 degrees Celsius (104°F) training ride. It was not one of his best decisions. Climbing Montseny he began to feel sick, and by the time we returned to the apartment four hours later he was bright red and in desperate need of a toilet. Due to construction in the streets the water in our Girona apartment was turned off, so he had to run down to the café each time he felt queasy. The water was back on in two days, and by that time he felt normal, but he has sworn never to drink *horchata* again.

Whitey almost eliminated himself from the Giro d'Italia after he attacked a seafood buffet before the prologue and ended up sick through the first week of the three-week race. In the Vuelta a Cataluña in 2002, he ate six full 8-inch long squid as an appetizer. He is a man of legend.

Chef Willy accompanies us on the grand tours to ensure we don't get sick from restaurant food and also to keep our diets nutritious and interesting. He makes different pasta sauces each day, risotto occasionally instead of pasta, and cooks up eggs for us prior to the stages each day. He is also a jovial guy and good for morale when we get tired.

Willy loves women and is a flirt. He'll know the whole female staff at the front desk of the hotel before we arrive and will already be working on figuring out who all the waitresses are and how old they are. He keeps us amused.

> *IT IS GOOD WILLY HAS SUCH A CHARMING PERSONALITY, BECAUSE HE NEEDS TO PUSH THE CHEFS ASIDE IN THEIR OWN KITCHENS TO COOK FOR US.*

It is good Willy has such a charming personality, because he needs to push the chefs aside in their own kitchens to cook for us. Rarely does he run into any difficulty with the hotel staff, but when he does, it's generally the bigger hotels that have insurance policies preventing strangers from working in the kitchen. In cases when he isn't allowed in the kitchen, he travels with a set of burners so he can always make us the pasta and post-race potatoes.

Spain has some of the cleanest kitchens with the nicest staff, while those in France tend to be dirtier and more run-down. The same observations can carry over to the rooms and hotels. Generally the hotels tend to be the best in Spain and the worst in France. In France we are often cooped up in small rooms, so small it is hard to have two suitcases open. While in Spain we often stay in brand-new hotels with beautiful rooms, high-speed Internet connections, and a well-stocked minibar for midnight snacks or post-race munchies.

Floyd Landis was the most colorful character on the team. He is ebullient and then fast asleep, on or off. He is talkative, and often says things before he really thinks them through or worries about who he might offend. Floyd is also calculating and serious when it comes to training and racing. He can be thoughtful and quiet, and he is a great teammate who always looks out for the other riders' interests.

I first met Floyd and raced against him when he was on the Mercury team in the late-1990s. He had just come from mountain biking and was racing on the road like he was on a mountain bike. He fell repeatedly, and always bounced back up after each crash, covered in road rash, getting straight back to the front to attack.

Floyd was raised Mennonite, so he has no knowledge of any popular culture prior to the time he left home in his late teenage years. So that means he has no idea of anything that happened in bike racing before Greg LeMond's 1990 Tour victory or any song or movie before MC Hammer or *The Lion King*. Perhaps that's what gives Floyd his carefree attitude and strong mentality. He doesn't seem to worry about what happened in the past, just about what is going on in the moment.

Floyd has a memory for music and can recall the lyrics to pretty much any song he has heard. On a two-hour drive to the airport, he sang along, word for word, with every song that came on the radio. Halfway through the drive I looked at our trainer, Pepe, and we just laughed. He knew the words to everything from Meatloaf to Anastasia.

In 2003 when Roberto Heras won the Vuelta for a second time, Spanish TV commentator and former professional cyclist Pedro Delgado came over to the table to congratulate Roberto and the team. Floyd whispered to one of the guys, "Who the hell is this guy and why does he think he can just walk in the restaurant and interrupt our dinner?" After Delgado left we explained that he was the 1988 Tour de France winner and one of the greatest Spanish champions.

During the Vuelta, Floyd's music kept us entertained while we drove to the races or hotels. He would mix everything from heavy metal to "gangsta" rap. Johan didn't like his choices much, but in my opinion it helped to have Metallica's "The Unforgiven" running through my head while we raced in the team time trial.

CHAPTER THREE

THE SEASON BEGINS

*T*he *first race of a new season* is always a shock to the system. The shift from a training bike and long group or solo rides to a race bike and an attacking peloton is always extreme and the body can sense it immediately. But by the second day of racing in 2004, my mind was back into it, the legs had come around, and although it had been a full four months, it seemed like just a week since I raced at the world championships in Canada in October of 2003.

The Volta ao Algarve, a race that takes place in February, is a nice event to start the season—the weather is warm in the south of Portugal, the racing is tame, and the undulating terrain of the countryside makes for enjoyable racing. The vegetation and environment feel similar to that of Southern California. The only downside to the race in 2004 was that the staff had to drive 2,300 kilometers (1,400 miles) to get to the start and then another 2,300 kilometers to get back to the north of Europe for the classics.

The race is comprised of five stages: three flat opening stages, followed by a 28-kilometer (17.4-mile) time trial, and then a hilltop finish
on the final day. During the early part of the cycling year, the riders
who are not racing in the classics tend to be racing in stage races in
Spain and Portugal where the weather is usually a lot better.

Lance had selected several early-season races with stages where
he could hone his fitness while also testing out new equipment. Trek
had done a lot of work to design an ideal time trial bike for him—the
fastest, most aerodynamic bike that would also be comfortable for him
to ride. To test the bike in race conditions, he needed to enter races with
long time trials. When the organizers found out he might participate in
their races, they often adapted the stage courses to suit his requests.

As in most stage races, the time trial and climbs are the major
deciding factors for the overall classification, the scoring system that is
based on the lowest accumulated time over all the stages. Therefore,
the tactic in Algarve was to ride conservatively for the first three days,
while staying out of harm's way, conserving energy, and not losing any
time. Floyd and Victor were both riding well at the start of the season
and were the most likely to have great rides against the clock and in
the hills, so the team protected them during the flatter stages.

We rode in the rain for most of the race, and at times the wind was
fierce and the rolling hills seemed relentless. The roads were so slick
we could feel the rear tires spin as we accelerated out of corners or up
hills. The sprint finishes in the rain were extremely sketchy, with
roundabouts and corners to be negotiated carefully. In the final kilometers, George Hincapie, Benjamin Noval, and Floyd Landis crashed,
but fortunately all three were okay, with only minor scrapes and

bruises. The good thing about crashing in the rain is that the slide is less abrasive and less punishing to the body.

Not many of the U.S. Postal riders mind foul weather. Lance revels in the rain when others cringe and freeze. On a rainy day, he is a hard man to beat. The team is full of tough guys who excel in bad conditions. From the classics to the alpine stages in the tours, we are not likely to back down due to adversity or foul weather. So the weather in the Algarve was not to our disadvantage—actually the reverse proved true since not one rider on the team was complaining.

It is always a bonus to stay at one hotel throughout a stage race, avoiding packing and unpacking and settling into a new environment each night. In the Algarve we were at a great hotel, close to the beach and near the soccer stadium built for soccer's upcoming 2004 European championships. The night we arrived, the stadium was being prepared for its opening night—a "friendly" match between England and Portugal. Our hotel hosted the English team's press conference and it was a zoo. The bar was packed and the bartender was very busy pulling pints. Reportedly the English team had 150 police officers at their hotel to protect David Beckham and the rest of the English.

Lance brought Sheryl Crow with him to the Algarve. She packed along her guitar and practiced while we were away racing. Sheryl is mellow and fits in well with the team. She doesn't mind eating a plate full of plain, overcooked, pasty-white pasta, watery salad, or bland boiled chicken—the typical race feast provided by the hotels.

On a few occasions during the race, Sheryl followed us in the team car with Johan, joking or encouraging us on the race radios. She often traveled to the races with us in the bus and never seemed obtrusive, but instead was thoughtful of all the staff and riders. But as we warmed up for the time trial, Sheryl was disappointed with our music selection, which at the time was limited to a collection of Elvis discs that belonged to our *soigneur* Alejandro, a huge Elvis fan, as well as a few Jim Croce discs. Good music, but not all that motivating before a half-hour all-out effort.

During the race, while coming back to the peloton from the team car with fresh water bottles, rain jackets, and long-fingered gloves for all the guys on the team, the Rabobank team riders were pointing toward our team car and looking at it while in deep discussion. When we reached the back of the peloton after negotiating our way through the caravan, one of them asked me whether that was Sheryl Crow in the car. When I answered yes, he quickly went around the bunch, excitedly, to find his teammates and tell them that Sheryl was in the race caravan.

There are rules that govern the race caravan, some written and some simply understood. Once a breakaway has formed ahead of the peloton and the gap grows to over a minute, the riders in the breakaway are allowed to call up their team cars for support. Once a team car is behind the breakaway, the rider will be able to call it up for water bottles, for food, or in the case of a mechanical problem or flat tire, for a replacement bike or wheel. The director in the car will also give the rider tactical advice and moral support. But when the peloton closes in on the breakaway and the gap decreases to under a minute, the cars are required to pull aside and leave their riders. The "one-minute" rule ensures that the cars don't get in the way of the peloton as it comes up from behind.

The same rule applies to the cars following the peloton: when riders are dropped off of the back of the peloton, the cars are stopped and a "barrage" is formed so that the dropped riders cannot use the draft of the cars to get back into the peloton. However, when riders have a flat, a crash, or go back to get bottles or food, the cars are allowed to stay behind the peloton and the riders can use the draft, to a certain extent, to get back up to the bunch because they have not been dropped due to a lack of steam. Race officials oversee the entire race from their vehicles at the front and back of the peloton, and essentially direct the team directors over the race radio

LANCE IS FAR MORE PROACTIVE IN THE RACES, AND IS OFTEN ON THE RADIO TALKING TO ALL OF US AND GETTING THE TEAM MOTIVATED.

on what to do and when. If the team directors do not obey the orders of the race officials, they can be fined and sometimes even thrown out of the race caravan.

Direction and motivation can also come over the radios, from fellow teammates in the peloton. Lance directs the team well and commands respect from the bunch. He is a good leader, not only of our team but also the entire peloton. He is an awesome champion, but he is still one of the guys when we're all together on the bus on the way to the race or heading back to the hotel. He leads the team much differently from a rider like Roberto Heras, for example. Roberto says few words to his teammates and simply lets Johan take command of the team. Lance is far more proactive in the races, and is often on the radio talking to all of us and getting the team motivated. While protecting him from the wind he stays right on your wheel so you never have to worry about looking back to make sure he is still there. Roberto was a tough guy to protect because he jumped around the peloton and didn't always stay with the riders who were protecting him. Both Lance and Roberto are champions and great cyclists, but Lance is a natural leader.

One evening during the race in the Algarve, we were sitting around the bar after dinner, drinking coffees and teas and chatting among ourselves about the race, the season, and the past off-season. A nice-looking young woman approached us with a cap and jersey, asking us for autographs as her husband waited for her a few feet away. She asked us how the race was going, where we were from, how we liked Portugal, and then told us that she loved our team, Lance, and the sport.

The next day at the race she came to the bus and asked to get Lance's autograph. When she saw him she was ecstatic, and it soon became evident that she was a fan of cycling because Lance had inspired her in her fight against cancer. She pulled off a wig to show him her hair loss due to chemotherapy. He encouraged her to keep fighting and hugged her. It was another reminder that Lance inspires millions of cancer patients and survivors to believe in themselves, overcome the odds, and win. Likewise, he has brought cancer to the attention of the cycling community.

The race in the Algarve ended well for the team. Floyd was flying: he won the final mountain stage in rain and hail alone, taking the overall victory. Victor was second overall and Lance fifth, and the team won the overall team classification as well. Although it was only February, the team already looked fit and worked as a solid unit. We had two wins prior to the Algarve race, both thanks to Max Van

GRAHAM WATSON

ALL IN YELLOW: *Floyd Landis took the overall victory at the Volta ao Algarve.*

Heeswijk who had won in the Ruta del Sol in southern Spain. U.S. Postal's teams in both the Ruta del Sol and Algarve were strong and successful, and by the time we left Portugal the team had five wins thanks to Floyd and Lance. It was our strongest season start ever. In 2003, we had only 12 wins for the entire year. We hadn't planned on being in flying form for these races because they were simply a buildup for the main objectives. With the victories under our belts, we were nicely positioned and feeling confident.

After the race ended, there were sandwiches, hot tea, and drinks for us on the bus. We enjoyed a quick, warm shower in the back of the bus to get most of the mud off our bodies before the bus and cars sped to the airport to catch flights home. I am always amazed at how fast everybody can get washed up, dressed, and all the stuff can get orga-nized and sent off in the right direction. There are cars going to Belgium, others to the airport, and others to southern Spain. The pieces always fit together and we are almost always at the right spot with the right bike and right suitcase. That's incredible when you con-sider all the details involved in the process.

From Portugal half of the team headed north toward the classics in Belgium and France, while the other half, me included, moved to the south of Spain for a single-day race in Almería and then a stage race in Murcia.

The coffee machine on the team bus mechanically burbled out another coffee as we readied ourselves for the start of another race. Shuffling down to the bus from our hotel rooms, we got in and assumed our spots for the ride to the start of the first stage of the Vuelta a Cataluña.

The first time I saw the bus, I was both impressed and nervous. It was my first trip with the team in Europe; we were heading to training camp in Javea, Spain, from the airport in Alicante.

"How do you like the 1980s strip club?" Christian asked.

The bus has a gray, blue, and red interior and exterior, is covered with logos on the outside, and lined with gray leather chairs with red trim on the inside. In the front there are 12 seats, two pair facing the front window and two sets of four facing each other with a table in between. The tables are rarely used for much other than a leg rest. Two long benches stretch toward the back of the bus, about 4 meters in length. After a race has ended and we're driving to a hotel, every seat is filled by eight riders and a director.

Lance always takes the corner spot on the back bench, a spot where you can see everything going on in the rest of the bus and also a comfortable spot where you can put your legs up. When he's not there, George takes that seat, and when George isn't there nobody else really seems to care who has it.

For some reason the Spanish guys always seem to sit in the front of the bus, sprawled over the chairs, whereas all the other guys like the couches in the back. In the 2003 Vuelta, it became the joke that the front half of the bus was for the guys doing well, Triki and Roberto, and the rest of us were at the back of the bus where we had been all day on the climbs. None of the seats on the bus are used in a normal fashion. Most of the time legs are up in the air, guys are stretched out, and bags of clothing are scattered. Some packs become pillows while others become footrests.

Everybody gets ready at the same time and the bus becomes a zoo. Backpacks of race clothing are opened, with gear spilling out—numbers, jerseys, shorts—everything that we need for racing. Riders punch the buttons of the coffee machine while others push to get to the race food. Sugar, milk, creamer, condensed milk, and stir sticks all sit beside the automatic machine. Luc and the *soigneurs* take care of the coffee machine, while the rest of us abuse it and demand that it supply our needs with no complaints, and when it doesn't, we call on them to remedy the situation. Cakes of different kinds—apple tarts, rice tarts, jam tarts, and small rolls or *paninis* filled with Nutella or jam—sit in paper bags next to the coffee machine. We can choose between a huge variety of Clif Bars, cakes, and Clif Energy Gels—all sugary and all fuel for the

ALL ABOARD: *Victor Hugo Peña and Floyd Landis relax in the bus.*

day's efforts. Sometimes they're hard to get down and other times they taste like the candy bars my allowance was saved for as a kid.

The cakes come from Belgium. They are ordered and bought by Freddy Viaene, our *soigneur*, from a local shop in his hometown— always the same quality and always the same taste. They're buttery and sweet, fresh, with a homemade taste, but also heavy and not ideal for a fast pace or a lactose-intolerant rider. We eat the cakes because they are high in calories, full of energy that we need to get us to the finish line without becoming hypoglycemic.

Cereals are packed away in the shelves of the bus for the trips home from the races. Soy milk, for the lactose-intolerant, is in the fridge beside the sweetened condensed milk for the coffee.

Tucked away in one of the storage bins on the bus is an ultrasound machine. In the early season it seems the ultrasound machine is always out and riders are lining up to use it in the *soigneurs'* room. While one rider is on the massage table, another will be sitting on a bed using the ultrasound on his knee while another rider roots through the food bin looking for a cookie or piece of fruit. MTV, CNN, or Eurosport is usually on the television as background noise.

In the bus there are also bags of ice and ice packs, which we tuck under our tights or place over our knees, necks, or any other part that aches from the race. It's not uncommon for us to be spread out across the body of the bus, nursing our aches in hopes of better muscles the next day.

The kitchen is beside the shower that is beside the bathroom. On the way to the races all of the doors separating the different compartments need to be closed, as the stench that comes out of the toilet is unbearable for the passengers. Most musicians have a "no number two rule" on their tour buses for good reason, whereas we pretty much have a bus so we *can* take care of number two before a race. On a bumpy, sinuous mountain road, the stench is even worse as the corners seem to stir odors up from the depths of the bus. The *soigneurs* do their best to keep the bathroom and shower clean, but there are odors they can't remedy, even with all the air fresheners and antibacterial sprays available.

MOST MUSICIANS HAVE A "NO NUMBER TWO RULE" ON THEIR TOUR BUSES FOR GOOD REASON, WHEREAS WE PRETTY MUCH HAVE A BUS SO WE CAN TAKE CARE OF NUMBER TWO BEFORE A RACE.

Cyclists are generally not clean and neat right before or after a race. The bus is a sty after everybody has scurried and pushed about in an effort to get ready. After the race all anybody cares about is consuming calories and putting their feet up. When we arrive at the hotel for the evening, from the front to the back of the bus there are wrappers and open empty cans and bottles rolling around on the carpeted floor. It was really nice to have Berry Floor as a sponsor—they would replace the carpeting when it became nasty with stains.

During the few years I spent racing with the U.S.–based Saturn cycling team, we had no bus or camper, so we often had an issue finding toilets prior to the races. In Europe riders duck behind buildings or bushes and nobody really seems to care, whereas at several races in the States the organizers penalize or disqualify riders caught peeing in the bushes. As a result, we frequently ended up simply using a water bottle in the team van prior to the start and then tossing the bottle in the garbage. PDM, the Dutch superteam of the late '80s and early '90s, was the first team in the peloton to get a bus. Prior to the PDM bus, teams used minivans and team cars to shuttle the riders to the start line and then to the hotel after the finish. Now every team in the peloton either has a bus or a camper van. It seems a necessity now, and it's hard to imagine how the riders managed before the bus.

The team buses, like the mechanics' trucks, often get shuffled around between teams. When a team folds, another team will buy its bus or truck, or when a team upgrades their truck, a team with a smaller budget might buy the old truck. All the vehicles end up getting worked over during the season. They are cleaned and well cared for but they do rack up at least a few trips around Europe throughout the season.

At Home in Girona

BY CHRISTIAN VANDE VELDE

The Girona chapter of the North American mafia got off the ground with our then-director Johnny Weltz in 1996. Johnny served as the U.S. Postal team director from 1997 to 1999. He was given the difficult task of getting a small American team into the Tour. He started this project, which gave Lance a vehicle for winning a record six Tours de France, in Girona, Spain.

Girona was an obvious choice for a European base town. It is close to an international airport (Barcelona), 40 kilometers (24 miles) from the beach, and has good roads for training. It also has good restaurants, and at that time it was inexpensive—but that was then. Lance now takes off from the Girona airport via his private jet, and the town's prices have more than doubled, for real estate as well as for a quick lunch.

The first pilgrims to reach Girona were team members Darren Baker, Marty Jemison, George Hincapie, and Tyler Hamilton; only George and Tyler still reside in Girona. Tyler left for a year in Nice but he came back quickly. So that means George is the residing mayor of eight years—and with his current contract it will be a decade.

I moved to Girona in the spring of 1998 with another American, Jonathan Vaughters. Luckily for me Jonathan speaks perfect Castilian, which helped us in venturing into the city from time to time, ordering pizza, and understanding when someone was really mad at us. JV and I moved into what was affectionately known as the YMCA.

The "Y" was a huge old apartment that, with some help, could have been amazing. But we didn't give it much help other than some loud electronics. It was called the "Y" because most of the U.S. Postal staff used it as their base. And it was free. So by the time JV and I took up residence, all the good rooms were taken. JV took the better of the two since he was older and wiser. In my "room" I could touch both hands on opposing walls at the same time, and when my suitcase was open I couldn't see the floor.

On the other side of the apartment, Darius Baranowski lived with his family—his wife, child, and mother-in-law. His mother-in-law didn't speak a word of English. She only seemed concerned with feeding Allen (the kid) until he burst. Then along came Juan (a mechanic) and Richard (a *soigneur*), and it was "Eight is Enough." Since then quite a few people have camped at the "Y," including Anton Villatoro, Julian Dean, Dylan Casey, Frank Hoj, and, of course, Michael Barry. Michael was lucky (or smart, I guess) and he only stayed for a week or two before moving.

There was no heat at the "Y." The linens were at least World War II–era. But these were things that we just accepted. We didn't have cars, scooters, cable, or much of anything back then. We always had this sense that it was only temporary and that we would soon be home in the comfort of the United States. Then the team became more and more established in Europe, so we started buying things that normal people have. George had maybe two bowls and a few knives; I had one knife but about 40 teaspoons. Our possessions were completely random. But we were all bachelors without many women to impress, so it didn't matter.

Jonathan Vaughters tried to clean once because his wife-to-be was coming to stay with us. He decided to throw some bleach in a bucket and mix it with water to mop the floors. We had to evacuate the premises for some time, and my sense of smell is still recovering, but there were no germs for many years. There are plenty of other stupid things that were done out of boredom or ignorance, like throwing water balloons at the people going to the show downstairs or filling up my new scooter with diesel instead of gas. The gas pump read "gasoil"—which sounds like gas, but no, it is actually diesel fuel. One of the many mistakes to be made by an American in Spain.

Lance moved from Nice to Girona in 2001 and with his stamp of approval, before we knew it, all the Americans were there and everyone was feeling quite at home. Freddy Rodriguez, Lance, and Tyler Hamilton all bought places that year and that really opened our eyes. I thought that they were crazy spending all that money on a second home in Spain. If I could only go back in time. By 2004, Levi Leipheimer, George, Lance, Tyler, Freddy, and I all owned homes in Girona. And in many ways I feel more at home there than in my American home in Boulder, Colorado.

By the end of 2004 there were close to 20 professional cyclists living in the area, some with their families. Most of us have brought our American homes with us, so to speak: American television, wireless Internet—all the things that make a home and make being away from family easier. George is still the mayor, and he now owns a new place with silverware, a wine fridge for the wine from his French fiancée, and a crib for his daughter.

The bus rolled into the center of town, inching its way down the narrow city streets, people gawking as we passed. "I can't believe we're going down into the city center in this bus," Christian said. "I guess everybody will know we're back in town." Christian had been living in Girona for a few years, and the town had slowly become a magnet for the North American riders based in Europe.

February 2002 was my first visit to Girona and my second time to Spain. We had arrived in Spain in the late winter as the team camp was held there instead of in California. Since then, the camps have always been in California, giving the North American–based riders an extra month in the United States. The bus had just driven us from Javea in southern Spain, the site of our January training camp, north to Girona where several of us would be living for the year. It was dusk when we arrived in Girona, and the temperature quite a bit cooler than it had been four hours south.

We pulled up to the pedestrian zone in the center of the old town, and the bus hissed to a halt. People stopped on their way home from work to stare at the bus with U.S. Postal billboards running down the sides. We pulled out our bikes and suitcases from the belly of the bus— everything we would need for our season in Spain.

George turned left toward his apartment, Christian, Dylan Casey, and I went right to our apartment, and Antonio, Dave, and Floyd stayed in the bus for the short drive to their apartment. We agreed to meet at the pizzeria in 45 minutes for dinner.

The narrow streets in the old town wind their way between tall, narrow apartment buildings that house storefronts at the street level. Each building is different from the next, some with fresh stucco, others with Roman walls from the fourth century. It took me a week to figure

WATERFRONT PROPERTY: *Girona is a home away from home for North American cyclists.*

out exactly where I lived within the walled city, which way the river flowed, and how to find all of my teammates' apartments.

The night air was cold and I felt a chill as we shuffled through the dimly lit alleys, by the shuttered shops, over the river that ran through the center of town, to the pizzeria in the plaza.

As soon as we walked through the threshold of the restaurant, all the patrons greeted Christian, George, and Dylan, asking how they were and welcoming them back to town. At 8:30, the restaurant had just opened its doors and was still almost empty. The chef was tying on his apron as we took our seats.

Christian's bright red baseball hat, my baggy jeans, and Dave's U.S. Postal team tracksuit contrasted sharply with the clothing that the Catalans wore as they trickled through the door throughout the evening. By the time we had paid our bill and were ready to leave,

TOWN HALL: *Girona is a maze of tall apartments and street-level cafés and shops.*

the other customers were just beginning to bite into their appetizers. Before parting ways and heading back to our respective apartments, we agreed to meet in the center of town for a training ride at 10 o'clock the following morning.

Dede and I now have our own apartment, not far from my first apartment in the center of town. Jonathan Vaughters passed the keys to us when he decided to leave Girona to continue his cycling career in the United States. We were fortunate, since it is in a beautiful old building that has been restored, and Jonathan left the apartment furnished. The landlady is a sweet older woman who always smiles and greets us warmly, asking about the bike races and other things I can't really understand because she talks to us in Catalan. I just keep smiling and nodding my head. Each evening she steps out of the apartment and runs errands in the town, picking up a small bag of groceries. Like clockwork, each night at 10 o'clock she double-locks the massive wooden front door to ensure that only the tenants can find their way into the building.

The routines of the town are comforting. The bells that ring above our apartment on every quarter of every hour at first kept me awake at night, but now the city seems empty when they don't chime. We have developed our routines as well. Pepe, from the hardware store below my apartment, leaves his cash register each morning to wave hello as I clip into my pedals to go training. Every second day we buy water from a small shop a block away—one pack of carbonated water and one flat. When Dede is away at her races, the neighbors ask where she is, especially the woman who sells Dede homegrown produce at the market and the folks at the health food shop where I buy almond butter.

Everybody knows we are cyclists. They all know Lance lives in town, that he lives in the old town, the Barri Vell. They see us walking up and down the streets, in and out of the cafés. They congratulate us when a race goes well and welcome us back after long trips.

Across from Lance's apartment there is a café owned by a kind woman named Judit. People have used the narrow street to get to the cathedral for centuries. Each time any of us walk by the café, Judit's warm welcome draws us to her patio where she serves us drinks, tapas, and lunch.

Girona is also a stopping point for the team buses, cars, and trucks as they head to the eastern side of the country for the early-season stage races, such as the Tour of Valencia, Tour of Murcia, and Semana Catalana. Before the races, hotels on the outskirts of town are packed as the staff rests up for the rest of the journey south.

The cars will leave for the start town of the race in the morning, and by midafternoon we're all loaded into taxis and heading toward the airport in Barcelona to travel to the same race. The team staff has already arrived by the time we reach our destination, and they take us to the hotel.

If Lance is racing at the same race, he will fly us in his own plane, which is easier in every respect and truly a luxury. We meet at the Girona airport where we are greeted at the door to the airport by the plane staff, and then we are escorted to the plane. The plane is parked within meters of the terminal and as soon as we get aboard, we are served drinks and snacks and provided with English magazines and papers, which we are all starving for since arriving in Spain.

The jet is similar to flying first-class on a commercial flight, with leather seats and all the amenities. But there are no other people, no lines, no baggage delays, or even baggage carousels to deal with. Generally the flights are short within Europe, between one and two hours. Jet lag is not an issue, and we can usually put some time in on the bikes before the flight or after we arrive at the hotel.

GRAHAM WATSON

JET SETTING: *Lance takes care of business while aboard his private jet.*

Often we will get up early, when the air is still brisk and the town still asleep, with the shops closed and cafés empty. George, motivated for the classics, came down to my apartment at 7:30 one morning prior to traveling to the Tour of Flanders, to ride my home trainer. I sat beside him and sipped coffee and answered e-mails while he pedaled away, eventually stripping down to his shorts and undershirt, his sweat forming a pool on the dining room floor.

George has been dreaming of the classics since he was a kid racing around Central Park in New York City. Each spring his motivation for the early-season events is high. He is meticulous with his training regimen, focused for the races, and determined to be successful. Training with him in the early months is tough as he is in incredible condition. After he rode on my trainer in the morning prior to his flight, he again jumped on his bike later that afternoon when he arrived in Belgium to ensure he didn't lose any fitness and stayed sharp.

George is a slick guy, a calm, smooth guy who is always well dressed, well groomed, and attractive to most women. His Web site guest book is full of the names of women who have written asking to date him or kiss him. But behind his image as a player and a ladies' man, he is a nice guy who has shown me the ropes in the pro peloton, pushed me harder while in training, and motivated me in the races.

George is now a father to a daughter named Julia who was born in the fall of 2004. In the spring of 2004, while training on the roads around Girona, George told me his fiancée, Melanie, was pregnant, and I can remember the smile on his face. He had found out while racing in Paris-Nice. He said that during the race he found a new focus and contentment. In Girona we have gone from being kids racing bikes, to married men, to fathers.

> BEHIND HIS IMAGE AS A PLAYER AND A LADIES' MAN, GEORGE IS A NICE GUY WHO HAS SHOWN ME THE ROPES IN THE PRO PELOTON, PUSHED ME HARDER WHILE IN TRAINING, AND MOTIVATED ME IN THE RACES.

Not only do we ride together, but many of our wives also ride through the hills around Girona together. Odessa, Levi's wife, was a professional cyclist for many years. She continues to ride several times a week to stay in shape and get some fresh air. She was also Sheryl Crow's main riding companion while Sheryl learned how to ride a racing bike for longer journeys. Leah, Christian Vande Velde's wife, is a great triathlete and rides daily, often starting out with us.

Dede also trained many times with George, Christian, Ryder, and me in 2004 to get fit for the Olympics. The extra effort she needed to hold on to our wheels in the hills put her in great fitness for the midsummer months' races. She sits on the wheels, breathing like a train chugging over a mountain pass. She will hold on for hours at an incredibly high intensity, impressing all of us with her strength and tenacity.

Usually the cyclists have left town and the wives are at home alone. One of the most challenging aspects of being a cyclist is leaving my wife home and traveling without her. But traveling with the team is much easier than being home alone. There is less downtime to focus on being lonesome, there is always someone to talk to while riding or relaxing in the room, and we always eat our meals as a group. My heart aches for Dede when the taxi takes off down the street and she is left alone for weeks, tears in her eyes.

The women do have each other for friendship and comfort. They are all going through the same experiences. Cyclists are not easy to live with, and it takes a strong, independent woman to marry a cyclist. We are gone over 150 days in the year, either at races and training camps or traveling. We train hard each day, nearly every day of the week, even at home. A day off needs to be spent resting, not walking around town to galleries or shops. We are expected to spend the entire season overseas, nine months of the year, in a foreign land, in a different home, away from our friends and families. We lead two different lives, we have friends overseas, and friends in North America. We have homes in two countries, two sets of dishes, two sets of winter clothing, two sets of summer clothing, and at least two languages.

At the beginning of the year, we are given schedules for the season. The calendars show where we'll be racing, when, what races we will focus on, and what races we will use to prepare for the team's goals. But during the year, the schedule often changes. Usually at least 10 riders are scheduled to do a race where only 8 can start, so all 10 pre-pare to race and then a couple of riders end up staying home as "reserves" to train for the next race. It is frustrating to the athlete who has to sit at home when he wants to be racing. We ride our bikes because we want to race. Nobody likes staying at home and training day in and day out for a race they don't know whether they will be participating in. But that is the way it goes, and once the rider has an understanding of this, he trains, gets ready, and then rides the best he can at the race so that he will be ready to do the next event.

Often, a few riders get sick, a few others get injured, and soon enough the team is looking for riders to start the races. Johan and Dirk schedule reserve riders for the races because they know there will be illness and injury to weaken the rosters.

Schedule changes are hardest for the wives and families of the cyclists. We travel so much during the season that whenever there is a small window of opportunity to have a weekend with the family, or a moment on the beach after a long stretch of racing, it is highlighted on the calendar and greatly anticipated. When schedules change, it can be heartbreaking for the person at home and equally as frustrating for the cyclist. But with time we learn to roll with the changes, adapt, and enjoy each moment we can spend together.

When I was a child, the garage at my parents' house in Toronto was a stable for bikes and scooters. The car never made it into the garage after my fourteenth birthday as it had filled up with bikes, skateboards, and vintage scooters. My father collects everything related to cycling as well as vintage Italian Lambretta motorscooters.

My dad was my first motorpacer. We would load the scooter and my bike into the back of our van and drive north of the city for a training session. We would unload the scooter and bike in the parking lot of an Italian café, and old men would shuffle out of the café to eye the scooter as we prepared for the ride. A 1950s' Lambretta is a rare sight, and a cyclist getting ready to ride behind one is even more bizarre. In very broken English they would tell us that they had ridden the same model of scooter in Italy when they were teenagers. As we pulled out, a cloud of blue two-stroke smoke blanketed the parking lot.

My father would get dressed up in a yellow jumpsuit, a cycling company's logo across his back, with an oversized open-faced helmet resting on his head. As the speed increased, the jumpsuit would puff up, making him look like a naked Homer Simpson, his helmet slowly inching its way to the back of his head until he noticed and pushed it back in place.

In Girona, our wives are the motorpacers. They know all the training routes we ride, where all the potholes lie in the roads, how to handle the scooter in the roundabouts, where to brake, and how much to accelerate. Levi's wife, Odessa, is surely the most stylish on her baby-blue scooter, her blonde hair capped by a peaked helmet.

Motorpacing is difficult for both the rider and the driver. Drivers must have a steady hand and knowledge of cycling and of the effort involved in riding. A small acceleration on the scooter translates into a hard acceleration on a bicycle.

Before a time trial, we often motorpace behind the team car to loosen up our legs and also to get a feeling for higher speeds. On rest days in big tours, we also ride behind the team car for a half hour to maintain a little speed and stay sharp and fresh.

It is virtually impossible to simulate a race without a scooter or car in front. While in the draft it is possible to ride at higher speeds, but also the effort is entirely different from riding solo. Behind a vehicle there are abrupt accelerations and decelerations, whereas without the vehicle the effort is steady. As a result it is nearly essential to jump in behind a scooter to physically prepare the body for the races. Ideally a motorpacing session is done at the end of a long ride or in the second half of a double day on the bike, since the athlete wants to simulate the race as closely as possible, and it is in the last hours of the race that the speed is the highest and the race the most aggressive.

Motorpacing sessions can be stressful on a relationship. In instances where wives and girlfriends are motorpacing their husbands or boyfriends, arguments can break out. It is stressful for a driver to have a cyclist on his or her bumper; the driver has to concentrate on the road in front, the speed, and then the cyclist behind. Behind, the cyclist is going hard and is uncomfortable about even minor things. A corner taken too fast or a hill driven too slowly can ignite the whole situation. The first time Dede paced me behind the scooter, she was in tears within meters of the house as the vintage Vespa scooter kept stalling when she accelerated and let the clutch out while pulling away from stop signs. Patience is key, and a lot of focus.

The exhaust from the scooter in front of me spits out oil and smoke onto my legs and shoes, covering me with black specks from my knees down. I am focused on the road ahead, the effort. I glance at my power meter to check my wattage, the amount of power I am putting out by pedaling my bike, and then turn my focus back to the rear fender on the scooter ahead of me and its proximity to my front wheel. The road veers, the scooter leans over, the kickstand nearly scraping the ground. The scooter accelerates moderately out of the corner, and I am out of the saddle, sprinting to stay in the draft and hold the speed. My heart climbs toward my anaerobic threshold as the road increases in gradient. I only focus on the road ahead—everything else becomes irrelevant as I try and hold the speed and maintain the effort.

My mind finds motivation in thoughts of racing. The harder I can push now, the better shape I'll be in for racing next week. I click my shifter down a sprocket and dig deeper. My legs begin to burn, and then a town sign pops into sight as I reach the top of the hill. One last effort. I shift down two more sprockets and accelerate hard around the scooter. The sign at the city limits is now my focus as I give everything I have to get to it as fast as possible. Chris, my friend driving the scooter, increases the speed and stays beside me, motivating me. I pass the sign and collapse on the bars from the effort, then reach down for my bottle and take a long pull on it, almost asphyxiating myself, as my body wants air as well as water.

We cruise back in through Girona, the scooter alongside me as I chat with Chris about the motorpacing session. As we reach the old town, I decide to do one more ascent of a cobbled wall that George and I would race up when he was preparing for the classics. The road is narrow and climbs through the cobbled city streets, by the cathedral, and eventually winds its way above the town. As we reach the bottom of the hill I accelerate, and Chris follows on the scooter, with a small pack of scooters alongside him. Around the first corner we hit the climb. I shift up and accelerate as the pitch increases. The scooters behind begin honking with encouragement,

Chris leading the orchestra. Tourists on the roadside cheer and a few kids make comments.

The top is in sight. I punch it over the crest, and my legs are done, aching with lactic acid and muscle damage. I coast down through the town and back to my apartment.

CHAPTER FOUR

SPRING FEVER

*T*he *2004 racing season* started off well for the team, as our team sprinter Max Van Heeswijk led the charge with several victories. I think Johan and Dirk had a running competition for victories during the first months of the year, as there are two race programs in the early season, one for the classics led by Dirk and one for the smaller tours led by Johan. Dirk has a quick advantage since he directs the classics riders and they are motivated to get results in the early part of the season. Johan follows Lance's program, with the majority of the Tour climbers who are slowly building their fitness with their sights set on the month of July.

For a good portion of the 2004 spring in Spain and all over the rest of Europe, the temperatures were frigid. Snow even fell on the vacation island of Majorca. Races were canceled and training sessions were done indoors on the home trainer and in the gym. It was certainly a relief when we arrived in Murcia in March in the south of Spain and it was warm and dry.

Going into the Tour of Murcia, our goal was to help Max out in the sprints and hopefully to win a stage, do well in the time trial, and maybe have one or two riders do well on the mountain stage. Winning the overall was too lofty a goal since many of the Spanish teams were flying at the time, notably the Comunidad Valenciana–Kelme team and the yellow-clad Saunier Duval squad.

Max is a nice guy who can unleash a vicious sprint. The journalists call him the "gentleman sprinter," because he is a polite, respectful sprinter. It's been my experience that most sprinters are arrogant and flamboyant, but Max is an exception. He started his cycling career racing in the dirt on a BMX bike and competed for the Dutch national team before switching over to road cycling when he reached the junior ranks as a teenager. He rode alongside Lance on the Motorola team and then moved to Rabobank, Mapei, and Domo–Farm Frites teams before eventually finding a home with U.S. Postal. He loves the ambiance within the team and is comfortable with the American mentality. During his first season with the team in 2003, he rode well, but in 2004 he became one of the most successful riders in the peloton, with victories from the start of the season to the end. He was the first rider on the team to win a race in the early spring and the last to win one in October. He doesn't like sprints that are the least bit nervous or sketchy—when riders are using their elbows to push others out of the way or forcing their way through holes in the group that are not large enough to fit a mouse. In a whirly finish Max will back off the accelerator to save his skin and his power for another day.

To set up Max, or any sprinter, for a sprint, it's necessary to keep breakaways from getting too much distance on the peloton during the race. It is essential that they are not too far up the road, so that we can reel them in with a team effort on the front of the peloton. Max must exert the least amount of energy possible during the race and must also arrive in the last 200 meters of the race in good position so that he can unleash his sprint without any difficulty. If Max has a straight shot to the finish line and nobody impedes his line, he is hard to beat because he not only has an explosive acceleration in his legs but also enough power to hold the speed for several hundred meters. Ideally, for Max to dominate a sprint, the finish needs to be slightly uphill.

The first test of the race at Murcia was the time trial. The field had many time trial specialists, and there was more depth than in Algarve. A few world champions, national champions, and grand tour time trial winners were included in the field. The course was a 20-kilometer (12.4-mile) loop on flat roads open to the wind with few technical difficulties. Lance brought the bus music for the time trial, some good stuff that had everything from Led Zeppelin to Limp Bizkit.

The coffee machine in the bus was putting out several dozen coffees before the race. A Spanish specialty is the *bombon*: a shot of espresso combined with about a tablespoon of sweetened condensed milk—a nice little boost of sugary caffeine before a time trial.

I figured I would give the time trial a solid effort because I had good sensations in Algarve the week before. So I had a team car follow me and a radio was pinned into the back of my skinsuit, so that our team trainer Pepe could communicate and motivate me. Pepe is Spanish, and he has a dry sense of humor.

As I passed riders in front of me in the time trial, he would tell me, "Okay, Michael, we pass the other riders with authority." That was a motivating boost that gave me a little extra mental gas as I passed my competitors staggered at one-minute intervals in front of me.

Prior to the time trial in Algarve my mom asked me why I was good in the time trials as a kid but had struggled a little more with them as an amateur and as a pro. I thought about this before the time trial in Algarve and couldn't come up with an answer other than that I wasn't going as hard as I had when I was a kid. As a professional I had always raced fairly well in time trials but never thought of myself as a specialist and therefore never had the confidence and drive to give it everything I had within me, both physically and mentally, to go as fast as possible.

Dave Zabriskie, a teammate at U.S. Postal from 2002 through 2004, and a specialist against the clock, told me you have to hit the bottom as quickly as possible, feel as much pain as possible, and go as hard as possible, and to keep "scraping the bottom" until the finish line. I tried to keep this in my mind, along with my mom's thoughts, as I rolled down the start ramp. To ride a good time trial is a science. It is essential to go as hard as possible without exploding; the effort needs to be tempered. The rider needs to focus on taking the corners fast and clean while accelerating hard after slowing down, the whole time staying concentrated.

In past years, the team has not had a sprinter who can win a race, or at least be the odds-on favorite in a sprint. In 2004, Max proved to the team that he could win the massive field sprints against the best sprinters in the peloton. So we began positioning him in the right spot for the sprints and he started winning races again. The sprinter needs to be in the draft of his teammates, or other riders, until the last moment when he can pound on his pedals and accelerate as fast as possible toward the finish line. He cannot use an ounce of energy too soon and must also time the effort exactly so that he does not run out of steam before the line is reached. Lance has rarely been involved in a sprint since he first won the Tour back in 1999. He is often in the first 20 placings, staying out of trouble and crashes, but is never on the front with the finish in sight. But in Murcia he was motivated to lead Max out.

With just over 1 kilometer to go, Pavel Padrnos was on the front, stringing out the peloton out into a single line and keeping any attacks at bay with Lance, Max, and me, in his draft. After Pavel finished his awesome effort

SCRAPING THE BOTTOM: *David Zabriskie pushes himself in a time trial.*

and had pulled off exhausted, I put forth a hard effort at the front, and then Lance took Max to the line. Lance went through the last corner at full speed without touching his brakes. At the line Max won by a good bike length over sprinting ace Erik Zabel, with the next riders coming across the line in single file.

It was an extreme adrenaline rush, and everybody on the team gave everything they had to get Max to the finish in a position to win. In the bus after the race, Lance was giving everyone high fives, and we were celebrating the exhilarating moment.

The most difficult stage of Murcia, and the one most interesting to the spectators, was on a course over a tough road with several climbs and a mountaintop finish. Daniel Rincon, our Colombian climbing ace with a perpetual smile on his face, even when it is pissing rain, cold, and muddy, was going to go for the stage victory and I was given the freedom to race for my own position overall.

Right from the start I knew that I was not having a good day; my legs felt empty and painful after each hard acceleration from within the peloton. I figured I might as well try and push through it and ride my own tempo up the final climb.

Lance held strong with the leaders for several kilometers of the climb, but then stepped off the accelerator to ride at his own tempo to the finish line. It wasn't really the time of year for him to be going into the red on a climb; his goals are later in the year. Murcia is a race to test fitness while racing to gain more fitness.

The Comunidad Valenciana–Kelme riders dominated the peloton right from the start of the stage, as they knew they had a potential winner in Alejandro Valverde, a young cycling talent who cannot only sprint but also climb. Rincon held tough with the leaders until the final kilometers of the long climb, when a flying Valverde left him.

Daniel lives in Duitama, Colombia, with his wife but spent the 2004 season in Spain, living with Victor. It was really inspiring to see how happy and appreciative Daniel was to be racing and to be a part of the team.

At dinner one night, Miguel Induráin, one of the greatest cyclists of all time, stopped by our table to say hello. Miguel is a quiet, unassuming guy, like most of the Spanish cyclists. He won the Tour de France five times through the early 1990s and remains a Spanish icon and hero to many of the riders racing in the peloton today. When he came to our table to shake our hands, Daniel was in awe, like a kid in a candy shop with bright, wide eyes. Miguel had raced with Daniel's

GRAHAM WATSON

MAD MAX: *Sprinter Max Van Heeswijk celebrates his winning stage.*

brother and was one of Daniel's heroes as a kid—to this day I think he is still Daniel's hero.

Murcia ended up being quite successful for the team. We accomplished more than we set out to, with two stage wins and a solid team effort. At the end of Murcia, U.S. Postal had the most victories of any team in the professional peloton, which wasn't bad considering we were the last to start the racing season as most other teams had begun racing at the end of January.

One of the trends I noticed in the first two races of the year was that we were racing as a team, unselfishly, for one common goal—with both Floyd's victories and Max's, everyone rode unselfishly, which is a great feeling and boded well for the future events. These races had not been marked as "goals for the season" but more as races to get in shape for the events to come.

From the warmth of southern Spain, I was scheduled to go to northern Europe, where I was quickly reacquainted with cold weather. So far I'd had a nice schedule; I only raced in the south of Spain and Portugal and didn't have to suffer through the frigid temperatures the rest of Europe was experiencing. In the south we had a lot of rain and were not getting suntans, but at least the races weren't canceled due to snow.

In Dwars door Vlandaaren, a one-day race in Flanders, I was initiated to the cobbles, the short, steep cobbled climbs—or *bergs*, as the Belgians call them—the wind, and the cold. All in all, it was a pretty good experience and one I would go back and fight through again. In 2004 we had a good team for the classics, as Max, Stijn Devolder, George, and Ekimov were all riding well enough to win any of the coming races.

Stijn is a young Belgian rider who loves to negotiate the cobbles and work as hard as possible at the front of the group. In fact, at times, we have to tell him to get off the front since he is either riding unnecessarily hard while towing the rest of the field along in his wake or he's hurting the rest of us because he is climbing too fast. Stijn is a quiet kid who loves his bike and his girlfriend. He studies the racecourses and results for hours every evening, and will then talk to his girlfriend for the rest of the night. On a bike he is versatile. He can ride the cobbles and climb medium-sized hills—a nice combination and a rare one.

Racing in Belgium on the cobbled roads is slightly insane—not only because of the decrepit cobbled roads, but the fight for position as we approach them. Riders use every available bit of road, dirt, sidewalk, or grass to get to the front of the peloton. A few times I found myself in front yards, dodging the fans standing on their lawns. For 200 kilometers (125 miles) I was completely focused, as if I was playing a video game: pedal, position, watch for obstacles, pay attention to tactics, eat, drink, pedal harder, get back to the front. At the end of the day I was tired, but left Belgium wanting more.

During Dwars door Vlandaaren, Ekimov, one of the essential cogs in the machine that is our classics team, crashed heavily and needed X-rays. It was later determined that he would miss out on the rest of the classics and would change his focus to the Tour de France and the Olympics. Ekimov has for years been the most experienced rider on the team and had raced in 14 of the last 15 Tours de France, only missing one in 1999 when his team did not compete.

He began his career on the track with the Soviet team, and then, after having achieved great success, he changed his focus. Since taking to the road, he's placed consistently in time trials, road stages, and classics throughout the entire season. At dinner he draws everybody's attention when he tells stories of his days racing in Russia, or his time with the Dutch riders in the early 1980s. After the Berlin Wall came down, he was one of the first riders to make the transition from the amateur peloton to professional ranks. In the USSR the cycling teams were run through the military, and while war was raging in Afghanistan during the 1980s, the cyclists raced not to go to war.

Literally they were told that the riders who placed well did not have to go to war, while the others were sent off to the battlefields. Riders in the peloton who crashed or had punctures burst into tears at the roadside, since they were essentially racing for their lives.

Eki is a man with a strong constitution. He pays close attention to his diet and training while also keeping his mind strong and focused. In 2002 he retired, only to realize he loves his bike too much to quit racing. He came back with the goal of defending his Olympic title in Athens, which he nearly did, only to lose the gold medal by less than 20 seconds in the last few kilometers of the race.

Two days after racing in Belgium I was sitting in the team truck for the short drive down to France and the start of the Critérium International. The Critérium is a race organized by the same group that organizes the Tour de France, Paris-Roubaix, and several other classics. The races organized by this group draw high-quality fields, with all the best competitors in the world, many of whom will also be the protagonists in the Tour during the month of July.

I drove down to the Critérium with the mechanics and the bikes, since it was the easiest travel option. It was quite fun sitting in the cab, listening to Creedence Clearwater Revival and chatting with the mechanics. It was the new truck's virgin trip so I was able to enjoy it while it still had the "new car" smell.

Northern France was not much warmer than Belgium and we started the first stage in leg warmers, thermal vests, gloves, and hats. The thermometer on my bike computer read 6 degrees Celsius (42°F)

as we headed off for our five-hour journey through the French countryside. We would travel through many of the battlefields our ances-
tors fought on in the two World Wars.

Several of the climbs we crested had date markers at the top,
telling the date the hill was taken back from the Germans. As the sun
shone on the fields it was hard not to think about all the lives that were
lost for our freedom.

The Critérium International is a short race, three stages in two
days, and a little less than 300 kilometers in total distance—less than
Milan–San Remo, the one-day Italian World Cup, as Floyd pointed
out. Despite this, it is a complete race with a time trial, a hilly stage,
and a sprint stage.

The first stage, the sprint stage, unfolded as expected with a solo
early breakaway gaining nearly 20 minutes, a chase ensuing from
behind in the peloton led by a few of the sprinters' teams, and then a
field sprint won by Frenchman Jean-Patrick Nazon from the France-
based squad AG2R.

After arriving at the hotel from the race at 5:00 in the afternoon, getting a massage, and eating dinner, Floyd did some quick math and figured out that, with the time change away from daylight savings, we had
nine hours until the next stage started. And it had just started snowing.

We woke up the next morning to clear but dark skies and shoveled down some breakfast. We watched the sun rise as we sat on the
frozen leather seats of the team bus on the way to the race. Sheryl was
awake, ready for the race, and was on the bus with a new disc she
played for us while we drove to the start. The photographers were also
up at the early hour, standing outside our hotel with their flashbulbs
going off as Lance and Sheryl came out.

At start time the sun was nearly fully up and the temperature was still below freezing. Riders had on skullcaps, leg warmers, scarves, and winter gloves to keep warm. The race started at the base of a climb, and as we ascended I thought we looked like a herd of cattle in the cold air of western Canada—steam rose off the peloton like cattle in a feedlot. It would have been amusing had we not been going uphill at an uncomfortably fast pace.

The wooded plateau region of France called the Ardennes is ruthless to cyclists. There aren't many flat or straight stretches of road. The stage was a short one at 100 kilometers (62 miles) and therefore stressful from start to finish. Our goal was to ensure that Lance and Floyd arrived at the bottom of the final climb in the front group and as fresh as possible. All went according to plan, and Chechu managed a nice fifth-place finish on the stage as well.

> AS WE ASCENDED I THOUGHT WE LOOKED LIKE A HERD OF CATTLE IN THE COLD AIR OF WESTERN CANADA—STEAM ROSE OFF THE PELOTON LIKE CATTLE IN A FEEDLOT.

The German Jens Voigt of the Danish team CSC made the Critérium International a major goal of his in the spring of 2004 and he didn't keep it a secret. We knew he would be one to watch, but we were amazed he was as strong as he turned out to be. On the climb he attacked and won convincingly over his teammate Frank Schleck. CSC had been riding well since the beginning of the spring and their winning streak was continuing. It seemed as if they won all the races they started in the first months of the season.

The afternoon time trial came upon us quickly, and before we could even eat our last mouthful of lunch we were back in the cars on the way to the race. Two stages in one day are challenging, and after racing in the early morning and then eating lunch, all the body wants to do is go to sleep. The trick is not to take a nap, because you'll feel even worse afterward.

The time trial was a short one, 8 kilometers (5 miles), on an undulating course with a few corners. I decided to race as hard as possible since I still wanted to improve on my time trialing, and the only way to do that is by practicing.

Lance, Floyd, and Chechu were all racing for the overall classification, and after racing as hard as possible they ended up finishing well overall. But, at the end of the long day of racing, a flying Voigt won the race by a whisker over Spanish time trial ace Ivan Gutierrez.

After two days of racing, three stages, cold weather, and some intense efforts, I was ready for a siesta back in Spain.

After the cold week in northern Europe I was hoping for a reprieve and some sun while racing in Spain, but it didn't happen. The Basque Country is renowned for its picturesque terrain, green hills, and cold, wet weather, so the chances of sunshine were slim. The Vuelta Ciclista al País Vasco (Basque for "The Tour of the Basque Country," also known as simply Pays Basque) is a five-day *hors categorie* UCI race, the highest level of race other than a grand tour, that many teams set as an objective for the early season and use as a trampoline to gain fitness before the Ardennes classics in the following week.

The racecourse is undulating and mountainous, with several climbs each day—25 climbs over the five days—with much of the distance covered on narrow farm roads.

We went to Pays Basque with loose objectives. Floyd knew he would be able to contend for the overall victory, but the rest of the team was still building its fitness for the coming weeks and months. So Floyd was our leader for the race, and the rest of us were left to race for him and try to finish well on the stages.

The Euskaltel team, from the Basque Country, carried the race throughout the week, setting itself up for the overall victory. The bright orange-clad team was either on the front keeping things under control or attacking to break the race up.

The Basques are fervent cycling fans. The climbs were consistently lined with fans throughout the week. Since we were racing through Easter week, I imagine most were able to get time off work to watch the race, but I was still amazed at the support there is for cycling in this region. Despite the bad weather there were more spectators than I have seen at most races in Spain, the Vuelta included.

The Basque region also produces and houses many of the top professionals in Spain—from Iban Mayo to Joseba Beloki to Aitor and Unai Osa. You can tell which riders in the peloton are from the Basque Country because they are usually quite fair-skinned in comparison to the other Spaniards, due to the cloudy, cool, and often rainy weather in the Pyrénées. The physical differences between the Basque riders and other Spaniards bring attention to a distinct bloodline that is no doubt a factor in the secession sentiment of the Basque region.

In the past year, I have noticed that the mullet hairstyle, short on top, long in the back, is coming back in force and can be seen throughout Spain and much of Europe. Many riders are growing out their locks as well. Dirk Demol seems to be going back to his 1988 Paris-Roubaix style, Ryder and I are returning to our Canadian roots with a few locks fluttering in the wind from beneath the helmet, and French former world champion Laurent Brochard's hair is finally in vogue again after two decades of patience.

During the race, Floyd refined his NASCAR look by including a mustache. It was blond and a bit sketchy looking, but he sported it throughout the week and into Paris-Roubaix, two days after *Pays Basque* ended. At the tops of some of the climbs, he had a little frost on it. We figured he might get a job on the police force when he retires from cycling, since they seem to be the only crew in the world to pimp the mustache these days. Not many riders make the transition from the hills in the Basque Country to the cobbles of Roubaix, but Floyd was motivated to race on the cobbles. He has

> WE FIGURED FLOYD MIGHT GET A JOB ON THE POLICE FORCE WHEN HE RETIRES FROM CYCLING, SINCE THEY SEEM TO BE THE ONLY CREW IN THE WORLD TO PIMP THE MUSTACHE THESE DAYS.

great bike-handling skills, which he perfected while he was a mountain bike racer, and he is comfortable on the ancient cobbled roads of northern France, the *pavé*, as the French have named them, so he was eager to help out the classics team in the north. During the 2002 Paris-Roubaix the conditions were horrible and riders were crashing on the *pavé* while riding in a straight line because the cobbles were uneven and slick as ice.

This time around Floyd was on the front of the peloton, keeping George out of the wind and in good position. As they flew over the stones riders were crashing around them, but George was focused on the wheel in front of him and on staying upright, while Floyd was constantly looking back to see if George was okay and still with him. Eventually George told him to just look ahead and make sure he stayed upright—wise advice.

The team has two buses, one small and one large. The small bus has seen as much roadway as the Steinbeck and Charley camper and has been moving pro teams around Europe for more than a decade. Conversely, the larger bus is similar to a rock band's tour bus.

The *buske*, as Richard, our Polish-born *soigneur* calls the camper-style Mercedes bus, was the Italian Gewiss-Ballan's team bus in the early 1990s. It has traveled across the mountains throughout Europe and has provided cover for many a chamois change. The little bus has seen better days but it still suits its purpose. And it holds the road well.

As snow fell hard, covering the road in a fresh blanket of white, Richard plowed the dutiful *buske* over the Basque mountain peaks. We were trying to get to the beginning of a stage of the Vuelta Ciclista al País Vasco. The start time of the stage was a couple of hours away and Richard glanced at his watch repeatedly as he drove through the blizzard. No other cars were passing us. In the back, riders grabbed hold of the armrests on the seats and stared out into the whiteness beyond the windshield of the *buske*.

Richard looked back at us as we sat nervously. Still not a car had passed the little bus.

"Hey guys, no problem, just a little snow," he said, trying to comfort us while focused on the trackless white road ahead. Every so often he glanced at his watch to see if we would make it to the race on time.

Floyd, nervous and angry, said, "Richard, take it easy man, this bus won't stop quick in the snow, and it is a long way down the side of that mountain. We're not going to be racing in this shit anyway, so there is no hurry. You don't need to look at your watch."

"Relaaaax. I am from Poland. This is just a little snow."

Exiting the bus, I glanced down at the *buske*'s bald tires. I was both impressed and horrified by Richard's accomplishment. But then my thoughts quickly turned to the imminent test of handling my bike in fresh snow.

After making it to the start I realized I hadn't ever raced in leg warmers in my career prior to this season. But since the start of the year, I had needed them on several occasions. It is not a fun feeling sitting in a warm bus, fully dressed to race, while watching snow blanket the windshield.

Thankfully the organizers had a little common sense and shortened the stage, and we started 50 kilometers (31 miles) from the finish, where there was no snow on the roads. But soon after the start, we began climbing and were back in the snow again. It was a day requiring good morale and warm clothes.

The North Americans filled out the top ranks of the classification in the *Pays Basque* as they had often done during the first months of the season. Lance, Floyd, Levi, Bobby Julich, Tyler, and George all rode really well, especially in the time trials. It was a spring that set the stage for an impressive season for American cyclists.

For the Ardennes classics, races held in the hills of eastern Belgium and the Netherlands at the tail end of the early-season classics, we were based in a hotel on the outskirts of Liège. The hotel was a bit of a biker zoo with several teams of riders cooped up, two riders to a small room, bikes and trucks jamming the parking lot and fans flowing in and out of the lobby looking for a photo opportunity with their hero or a free hat or team water bottle.

The Ardennes week—when the Amstel Gold Race, the Flèche Wallonne, and Liège-Bastogne-Liège all take place over eight days—marks the transition in the season from the flatter, cobbled races to the hillier races. Some of the riders from Paris-Roubaix will push through until Amstel, but few will go all the way through Flèche and Liège.

> THE COBBLED CLASSICS ARE DAMAGING TO YOUR BODY. I HAVE ONLY RIDDEN ON THEM A FEW TIMES AND THE NEXT DAY I FEEL LIKE I HAVE THE FLU COMING ON.

The Flèche Wallonne essentially signals the shift in the calendar, when the riders aiming for the Giro d'Italia in May start to fly, where the Tour de France riders start to really improve, and where the climbers come to the fore. The peloton morphs as well. The riders in the Ardennes classics are smaller, with a lot less muscle mass, and are far less aggressive in the crosswinds. Most of the Paris-Roubaix riders are tired from a hard spring and taking time off to recover from the stress of the races.

The cobbled classics are damaging to your body. I have only ridden on them a few times and the next day I feel like I have the flu coming on. My body aches all over, and getting out of bed is a bit of a chore. After the 2004 edition of Paris-Roubaix, I remember trying to talk George into coming to Amstel, since it is a race that could suit him as he was riding well. He was in France spending some time with his fiancée, Melanie, and her family. On the phone he sounded horrible and told me that he had napped all day and still felt like a truck had run over him. Racing can't be healthy when it makes you feel sick, which it usually succeeds in doing when you spend too much time riding beyond your limits in horrible conditions.

It was my first time competing in these three classics and I gained some valuable knowledge. Positioning in the peloton is quite important, as the climbs tend to be on smaller roads where it is hard to move up, and if a rider sits up or can't hold the wheel, a gap opens quickly and it is hard to close it in time. Even a meter can be impossible to close. This is how the peloton splinters and why positioning is crucial to success in the Ardennes classics. Flèche and Liège are also fairly technical races, with many corners, roundabouts, and traffic islands. Being in front makes a huge difference because the back of the peloton often comes almost to a standstill on corners, producing the proverbial rubber band effect.

Flèche was one of the fastest races I did in 2004, and amazingly faster than most of the criteriums I did while racing in America, with an average speed of 47 kilometers per hour (29 mph). It was hard to believe we went that fast because the race is nowhere near flat, there was not a constant tail wind, and the race was 200 kilometers long.

At the start of the race, the field split in two on a flat section of open road, and we ended up chasing in the wind for 35 kilometers since most of our team was in the second group. In the group with us was Italian Davide Rebellin of the Gerolsteiner team, who ended up winning at the end of the day. Had we not chased the front group down, he may not have won the race, but that is bike racing.

Two days prior to Liège we went toward Roubaix to preview the Tour de France stage that ran over some of the cobbled roads in the area. There are two sections that the Tour was going to pass over and Johan wanted to make sure the team previewed them so there would be no surprises during the Tour de France. I think the highlight for most of us was getting the chance to ride the Arenberg Forest sector of cobbles; it is perhaps one of the hardest sectors in the Paris-Roubaix. We were like kids in a sandbox when we got to the forest, riding up and down the road repeatedly, laughing and joking. It was a good training ride and got us out of the hotel for the day, something we all needed.

Having never competed in Liège before, I figured it might be a good idea to ride over the last climbs of the race in training. Saturday, we rode the last 50 kilometers of the course, from La Redoute to the finish. It was good to see the climbs and find out what to expect in the next day's race. The climbs themselves are not that difficult, but they come one after another in the last hour of a six-and-a-half-hour race.

The night before the race, as we were all sitting down and stuffing our faces for the coming day, Ulrich Schoberer, the engineer/designer/owner of SRM power meters (a bicycle computer we all use for training that allows us to gauge our efforts through our produced wattage and heart rate readings), sat down to eat with us and chat. He pointed out that we shouldn't worry about eating too much as Liège is the hardest one-day race on the calendar since it requires the greatest kilojoule expenditure (a kilojoule equals about 1.3 calories). Uli has data files on the best racers from nearly all the classics. He figured Liège would be a 7,000-kilojoule day. Having had stomach problems throughout the week and having not digested much of my food, that didn't bode well for me.

We rode Liège in much the same way we had ridden the previous races in the week. Floyd was our leader, while José, Triki, and Chechu were free to ride their own race and the rest of us were to keep them in position and well fueled.

At the end of the long day in the saddle, the outcome of the race was similar to the previous races that week: Rebellin was victorious again for his third time in the three races, Michael Boogerd of Rabobank was second, and the peloton stayed together until the last moments of the race as the speed was fast but controlled for nearly the entire race.

I was impressed with the crowds and support we had during the week of racing. Each climb—and we went over too many to count in the weeklong period—there were spectators packed along the sides, as well as on each corner and through the towns. I left the week wanting more, wanting to race the races again, as I had a clearer picture of how they unfold and how it is tactically best to race.

CHAPTER FIVE

THE PSYCHE OF CYCLING

A hard bang on the door wakes me up. The hotel room in Liège, Belgium, is dark, and light has yet to even peek through the crack in the curtains. Chechu wakes moments later as the banging continues.

We yell, "Yeah, what?"

"The UCI is here," the knocker responds.

Damn. We switch the lights on, squinting at the brightness, and stumble around to find our clothes. This scenario could play out at any race at any point in the season, but on this particular morning we are to start Liège-Bastogne-Liège and we have a half hour to go downstairs to have our blood tested by Union Cycliste Internationale inspectors.

We arrive downstairs to a long line of riders. There are four or five teams staying at the same hotel. About 30 of us are hanging out in the hall, some are sleeping again, others are quietly chatting, and everybody is tired. We wait in line. It is quite an early-morning sight for all the tourists in the hotel to see the best athletes in the sport sitting on the floor in a hallway of a hotel while their teammates file out from drug testing. Riders come out of two rooms, one on either side of the hallway, holding their forearms and applying pressure to a small piece of gauze. I am all for drug testing and health checks, but it would be nice if there was a little more privacy offered to the athletes during tests.

At a random drug test in Canada four of us on the national team were told by the person testing us that "they would nail us all eventually." She then realized what she had said, when we opened our mouths in astonishment, and said, "Well, I mean, we'll eventually test you all anyway." It doesn't give you much confidence in the system when the testers come across as though they are out to get you.

> AT A RANDOM DRUG TEST IN CANADA FOUR OF US ON THE NATIONAL TEAM WERE TOLD BY THE PERSON TEST-ING US THAT "THEY WOULD NAIL US ALL EVENTUALLY."

Four times a year the UCI, cycling's governing body, demands that all riders on the top 50 teams ranked by points accumulated throughout the season's races, have their blood tested. These tests are not random, like the one in Liège. Registered laboratories run comprehensive tests, including everything from hormone analysis to checking for ferritin, or iron stores. The tests establish whether we are all healthy to race and within normal test values for an average male. It is good to monitor all of these values since a cyclist is often depleted from training and racing daily or he may be sick. Tests of the blood can also reveal banned manipulations, such as the use of synthetic hormones or blood transfusions.

The UCI checks our health prior to races to ensure we are within safe blood limits. If we are over the legal limit of a 50 hematocrit, 17 hemoglobin, or have a reticulocyte count that is off, we are suspended from racing for two weeks. These tests were put in place at the end of the 1990s because of the prevalence of blood boosters within the peloton. Erythropoietin (EPO) is one such blood booster— it promotes the formation of red blood cells, increasing the oxygen-carrying capacity of the blood.

After each race we complete, a handful of riders are tested for banned substances. The race winner, the race leader (if it is a stage race), some of the riders who have placed, and random riders in the peloton are selected for a urine test and a blood test. The selected riders must show up to a mobile lab immediately after the race and give their samples in the controlled environment. During the Tour, for instance, Lance will be tested a dozen of times, as he is tested if he wins a stage or is wearing the yellow jersey. During the season we are all tested frequently both at the races and at home.

Each quarter of the year we are asked to provide our home address and whereabouts at all times during the upcoming three months so that we are available for out-of-competition testing. Our mobile phones are always on so that we can be contacted while out at dinner or while away from home, as three missed tests brings a penalty of non-participation at the Olympic Games and a possible suspension.

As I was sitting in the hotel hallway with one of my teammates at Liège-Bastogne-Liège, he commented how we get our health checked constantly by the UCI but they are less concerned with protecting our safety in the races. Cycling is inherently a dangerous sport, but it has become more dangerous in the last 15 years. The races have become faster, the pelotons are larger, the roads are busier with traffic and traffic islands, and roundabouts and traffic-diversion devices are becoming more common throughout Europe.

Just days before we arrived in Liège, we were dodging parked cars at the Flèche Wallonne, one of the premier races on the calendar. We also raced on an incredible, technically dangerous course at the Amstel Gold Race. I can understand the spectacle of the race and the fact that sinuous courses on small roads or in city centers are interesting for the public and make good television, but it doesn't take much for one rider to hit a pole or a curb, ending his career or perhaps his life.

> SINUOUS COURSES ON SMALL ROADS OR IN CITY CENTERS ARE INTERESTING FOR THE PUBLIC AND MAKE GOOD TELEVISION, BUT IT DOESN'T TAKE MUCH FOR ONE RIDER TO HIT A POLE OR A CURB, ENDING HIS CAREER OR PERHAPS HIS LIFE.

Although the organizers of *Pays Basque* relocated the start of its snowy stage, we started races in the snow several times in 2004. The organizers always want us to race no matter what the weather, because the sponsors of the race—as well as the start and finish towns—have a vested interest in the race running as planned. Racing in the snow on mountainous roads with a large peloton is not safe for obvious reasons, but our safety sometimes seems low on the overall list of priorities. When races are canceled due to unsafe circumstances, it is usually brought about by the riders refusing to participate, rather than the organizers looking out for the safety of the event.

During the 2004 Tour of Belgium the racers took a stand as they approached a dangerous finishing circuit and stopped racing. The organizers were appalled that the peloton would come to a halt and insinuated to the media that riders of previous generations would never have stopped the racing. From a rider's perspective it was really good to see the peloton come together and take a stand for its own safety and health. The same type of thing has happened a few times in America in recent years. Hopefully this will become a trend, and when our lives are at risk, we won't all just follow the *commissaire*'s car like sheep going to slaughter.

In the 2002 Vuelta I was involved in a crash that is often described as horrific. Five of us crashed while going down a mountain at over 60 kilometers per hour (37 mph). The crash itself didn't injure me too badly; but a motorcycle coming from behind caused more damage. The motorcycle, carrying a television cameraman, came to a grinding halt with my chest under its front wheel. I was dragged for about 30 meters along abrasive pavement, tearing my skin and breaking my bones.

After everything had come to a halt, I opened my eyes to see the front suspension of the motorcycle right in front of my face and on top of my chest. For months after, as I was recovering at home, I would wake up sweating with that image impressed in my mind.

I got up from the crash and soldiered on to the end of the stage. It was adrenaline and the thought of not being there the following weeks for my teammates that kept me going. The other riders in the *gruppetto*, the group of dropped riders behind the race leaders, nursed me through the stage, offering me water and giving me a push on a climb or out of a corner.

It wasn't until I reached the ambulance at the finish line, when a gaggle of journalists swarmed me, clicking photos and asking me questions as if I had just won the race, that I realized how bad my injuries were: I was covered in road rash and my ribs were aching.

I rode to the hotel in the bus with Johan and Dirk, standing up for most of the ride because I couldn't sit with road rash covering my body from head to toe. After discussing it with Johan, Dirk told me I wouldn't be starting the next day. That was devastating, but I also knew it wasn't going to be possible to even get my leg over a bike the next morning. It took the doctor and Elvio, a *soigneur*, an hour and a half to clean me up. Elvio, a cool Italian, dryly commented as he applied bandages to the burns on my chest, "That motorcycle had a good tire on it. You can see here that it was a Pirelli." I cracked a smile.

Weeks later Dede counted 36 big cuts on my body.

Two days prior to my crash, we had been descending an incredibly fast bit of highway at 80 to 90 kilometers per hour (approximately 55 mph), when Matt White pointed out a motorcycle cruising in the middle of the peloton a few feet from the riders. When things settled down he said, "What the f— is a motorbike doing in the middle of the peloton at 90 kilometers per hour? Doesn't he realize that if there is a crash he'll kill someone with the 1,000-pound bike?"

A week after my crash, two motorbikes hit each other and caused a massive pileup, ending the race for many riders. I understand that the motorcycles need to be among the riders during the race to give the race media coverage, but sometimes the drivers take huge risks and don't realize the danger they put us, and themselves, in. Sometimes I think they forget it's only a bike race.

Every cyclist in the professional peloton has had a bad crash. We all have battle scars on our elbows, hips, shoulders, and knees.

GRAHAM WATSON

CARNAGE: *The motos go down at Paris-Roubaix.*

Crashes are something nobody talks about. They happen, it's part of the sport, and it's unlucky to talk about them. I say a prayer every time I see one, every time there is a near miss, or every time I hear bikes hitting each other or the ground.

There is a quick moment just as you get caught in a bad situation where you try to save yourself. Sometimes you can stay up and keep going, while other times you can't and simply prepare yourself for the fall. It is this moment that flashes through your head for weeks after a crash. That moment stays with you for a long time.

Dave Zabriskie has had a few horrendous crashes. He told me that when he closes his eyes he still sees the bumper of the SUV that pulled out in front of him while he was descending during a training ride near his home in Salt Lake City in May 2003, breaking his leg and wrist. The image will probably stay with him for the rest of his life, as will the scars.

The challenges of the sport constantly push competitors to their limits, compromising their immune systems and forcing them to take risks on the road. Often it is necessary to push beyond your limits to win, but sometimes there is a heavy price to pay. Frequently at least one guy of the 20 or so on the team has some kind of health problem and cannot race or ride. Whether it is a saddle sore, which forced me to stop the 2004 Tour of Belgium, a crash, a cold, or some kind of virus, there is always something keeping us from riding.

In 2003, the team was riddled with injuries, colds, and problems. The entire spring became a write-off, since we constantly started races with one or two riders less than other teams. It is one thing to lose a rider in a race but another to start with fewer riders. On the team, as well as among the cyclists from Girona to Boulder, it is common to hear of riders nursing injuries whether they are from a recent crash, a crash earlier in their careers, a boil, a cold, or an uncomfortable stomach.

Almost every member of our team has had a bad crash at one point and now suffers as a result in some way or another, whether it is an ache or pain, an imbalance, or mental stress. Cycling daily for hours above your lactate threshold in rain or snow is not healthy. Cycling is a healthy sport if one rides daily for an hour or two, maybe three or four on the weekends, but taxing your body for weeks or months, season after season, wears it down.

But athletes are skilled at blocking out pain. It is part of sport. Our bodies become resilient and our minds develop the ability to ignore pain, whether it is from racing as hard as possible or pain from sore legs, a patch of road rash, or an aching back. In fact, I cannot even remember where and when I obtained most of the scars that are strewn across my body, covering my knees, elbows, chin, back, bum, and hands. There are a few bad accidents that really stand out in my mind, but I have blocked out many of them and others just run together in my memory. I am always amazed at the body's ability to recover.

To ease the pain we have massage therapists who travel with us, keeping us nimble, aiding in our recovery. The *soigneurs* make sure we have all the right foods at breakfast in the morning and in our pockets for the races, and get us from the hotel to the start and back from the finish each day during the races.

The *soigneurs* have all the creams to keep us warm in cold and rainy races, to keep our butts comfortable on the chamois, and to block the sun. They have all the patches and tapes we need to cover the weeping wounds and clean a cut. They usually have whatever we need on hand. If not, they'll make sure we have it before the day is over.

For the new riders on the team an injury is the worst possible problem. The natural instinct for a young rider is to want to prove himself to the team directors and his teammates; therefore, the plague of an injury is traumatic. He cannot ride at the level he had hoped and often permits the stress of being injured to eat him from inside. For instance, when I first came to the team in 2002 I had an injury from lifting weights. It wasn't healing with rest or ice or ultrasound, and the pain never ceased. I didn't want to tell anybody on the team how bad it was for fear that I would not be able to race. I waited as long as possible to tell Johan and the doctors that I did in fact have a problem and that I hadn't been able to train properly. I was worried they wouldn't understand and simply put me on the shelf for the season, but I was wrong. My race program was changed, I was able to recover, the doctors

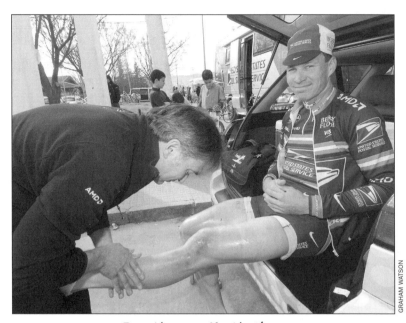

GRAHAM WATSON

THE RIGHT STUFF: *Freddy Viaene gives Max Van Heeswijk a rub.*

treated me, and I was back on track soon enough. Although the team is there to help the riders, the riders also have to help themselves by being honest and realizing when the injury should take precedence over trying to race. It's something that we all learn with maturity.

In spite of all the aches and pains, we continue racing and training. It is very hard to get a cyclist to stop. The online reports don't tell of all the injuries riders are enduring through the weeks of a race unless they are serious. Riders keep quiet about it, plow on, and think of nothing but the finish line, tomorrow's stage, the last week of the race, the trip home, or the next hill. Push the pain out and keep the legs moving.

Because cycling is an addiction, the hardest thing for a cyclist to do is to take time off to recover from an injury. The first thought is to not lose fitness, and then there is that desire to release endorphins, to exert your body. Sitting on a couch makes an athlete irritable and easily annoyed. An innate desire to be fit and ride consistently develops in nearly every cyclist.

In 2002, we had finished a 10-day-long training camp and were tired from the efforts in the mountains and high pace on the flats. As we were getting ready to head home Antonio Cruz asked Lance what he thought he should do for training in the coming week. The expected response was a few days of rest, but Lance said, "I would ride my bike, because I just love to ride my bike."

During the 2002 Vuelta, the peloton split into groups on the first climb of the race, the first road stage of the race, with another 20 stages to go. We had just left Valencia and were climbing out of the seaside town into the mountains. The peloton had shattered behind the front group of 30 riders, and several of us found ourselves fighting to get back in contact with the front.

Roberto Heras was our team leader for the race, and he had the fitness to win. He eventually did go on to lead the race up until the final time trial in Madrid, when Aitor González took the lead. The sole objective for the team in the Vuelta was to protect Roberto and ensure he would get to the mountains in the front, and then to keep the race in control. It was not a good sign when we hit the first climb of the race and several of us were dropped from the peloton as we could not follow the leaders' pace. Antonio Cruz, Steffen Kjaergaard, and I were riding with everything we had, on the tips of our saddles. On a descent

Antonio slid out and hit a steel guardrail that, thankfully, was there, or he would have fallen a long way down the mountainside. He got back up in a hurry, changed his bike, and got going again to try and get back in the race.

When we arrived at the hotel after the finish, Antonio's leg wasn't looking too good. He had a gash on his thigh four inches long and very deep. It looked as if he had been slashed with a knife and fallen out of a moving vehicle.

Antonio is used to road rash. He's been racing since he was a teenager and has done a lot of criteriums in America, where it is inevitable that a rider will have a few bad crashes. Antonio shrugs off road rash as if it's a paper cut. The cut on his leg was not road rash and it was certainly a lot worse than a small paper cut. All the riders on the team came to check out Antonio's injuries and were slightly in shock when they saw the gash on his leg. The team doctor came in to take care of him.

NOT WANTING TO GIVE ANTONIO ANY ANESTHETIC FOR FEAR THAT IT WOULD AFFECT HIS PERFORMANCE THE NEXT DAY, LUIS GAVE HIM A PIECE OF CLOTH TO PUT IN HIS MOUTH AND PROCEEDED TO SEW UP THE CUT.

"We have to sew it up," Dr. Luis del Moral said to Antonio.

Luis doesn't have the best bedside manner. He is terse and to the point; he likes to get the job done and he doesn't like it when we cringe. Not wanting to give Antonio any anesthetic for fear that it would affect his performance the next day, Luis gave him a piece of cloth to put in his mouth and proceeded to sew up the cut. Dave Zabriskie, Tony's roommate, turned his head and cringed as Antonio's eyes welled up and he bit down into the

Health, Superstition, and Central Air

BY GEORGE HINCAPIE

The bus is great for getting to know teammates from different countries; each person brings his own culture and background to the experience. When we travel to races, we usually bunk two teammates to a room. When you room with someone from a different culture or background, there can be some pretty funny ideas that come to the surface. For example, even though some of the days during the Tour are really hot, some European roommates refuse to let me use the air-conditioning in the room. They insist that the AC can make you sick. They even feel that having the window open can make you sick, too. The whole time I was at the Tour I remember thinking that not being able to sleep in the heat was going to affect my performance.

My teammate Viatcheslav Ekimov, who is a great friend, never let me turn on the fan when I would room with him. He said that fans make you sick because they stir up the germs and bacteria in the room. Meanwhile, we're racing over 100 miles a day in the heat and rain and cold in all kinds of conditions, and he thinks that is okay? But the Europeans continue to insist that sleeping with the AC on, or the windows open, or the fan on will make us all sick for sure. Even with all the different ideas about what makes for a healthy and strong race, we pull it together and race hard every day.

cloth. Every muscle in his body tensed up as the needle and thread went in and out of his skin.

There were still 20 days to go. Antonio finished the race and was able to help Roberto all the way to the time trial in Madrid.

In cycling, as in many other sports, superstitions plague or inspire the athletes. A lucky number can motivate a rider while an unlucky number can immediately take the air out from under his or her wings.

As a child, when I was first starting out in cycling, I had several superstitious patterns—after a victory I would stick with the same jersey and shorts and the same gloves for the next events. My coach as a junior would take the numbers we were given for the start and through them predict which place we would finish in the race. A good number was 21, as two minus one is one, implying that the rider would be first. For a long time I would always start a race in the big chainring. If we started on a steep hill, I would immediately shift down as soon as I crossed the start line, since for some reason I thought that was lucky.

At the dinner table each evening, salt is never passed from person to person, hand to hand. Instead, it is placed on the table for the next person to pick it up, a superstition that most of the European peloton adheres to. Triki, however, is more concerned about the salt being passed around, or even worse, spilled, than anyone else on the team. Lance won't accept a saltshaker until it is put on the table, but Triki worries for the rest of us when we pass the salt to each other. In 2003 when he joined the team, he made it clear that salt was not to be passed. Once when it was passed, he blamed Chechu's crash the following day on the salt. When salt is spilled at the table, Triki immediately throws salt over both of his shoulders, often leaving the table looking like he has a bad case of dandruff as salt rests on the black fleece top that he wears.

In the peloton, team cars that are ranked thirteenth in the race caravan flip the 13 upside down when the director is superstitious, and the same is done with frame numbers on the bikes or race numbers pinned to the jersey if the rider is worried about bad luck.

We never talk about crashing or about our injuries. Talking about falling brings bad luck. In the Tour of the Algarve in 2003, Zabriskie was rooming with me, and the night prior to the first stage he said, "Okay, let's not crash tomorrow and break the curse of Michael." Dave had developed a theory with our teammate Robbie Ventura that I was bad luck and those who roomed with me crashed. The superstition started after Robbie had crashed twice while rooming with me.

After Dave brought up crashing and breaking the spell, the forecast was grim for the next day. I had a bad feeling we were going to crash, not because I was in the same room with him but because he had spoken about crashing. We both ended up crashing, but perhaps because of the double crash, the curse was broken. Dave was out of the race and spent the rest of the week playing games on his computer in the hotel room while the rest of us were away racing.

While traveling constantly and changing rooms, race clothing, numbers, and environment, it is difficult to stick with the lucky charms and avoid the unlucky. I realized as I left the junior ranks that the lucky jersey and shorts didn't really help me much, that I could win no matter what number I had on my back, regardless of whether I started the race in the big or little chainring.

While racing in the United States, I am selective about what I do and do not eat. I avoid too much red meat and eat organic foods as much as possible. At races we eat breakfast in our rooms, having bought the food the day before at the local market, and then for lunch and dinner we try to find a health food market or quality restaurant. When we are in Europe I eat what is in front of me at the hotel. Nobody on the team has any major food hang-ups or special dietary requests. Dave Zabriskie will not eat red meat in Europe because he is worried about BSE, or mad cow disease, and Benoit doesn't eat any fruits or vegetables at all unless it is in the form of jam or candy, or potatoes or pasta sauce. Otherwise, everybody eats what is put in front of him, as the choices are pretty slim otherwise. The hotel has a menu, Willy cooks up the pasta at the Tour, we have a plastic box full of cereals, jams, and cookies, but there are no other options. It would be hard to be a vegetarian and race in Europe for a full season, since there are few protein sources other than meat available to us.

There is a scale in the hallway when we arrive at the hotel so that we can weigh in and gauge whether we need to eat more or less. We also try and weigh ourselves after the races, to see how much water we've lost and therefore how much needs to be replaced. As soon as the *soigneurs* arrive at the hotel, the scale is put in place. Some of the guys walk down the hall in their boxer shorts or underwear to get the most accurate reading.

Diet is a big part of being a good cyclist. Benoit Joachim has the most shocking diet of any of the riders. He consumes a jar of Nutella (a hazelnut-chocolate spread) in a day or two at breakfast and also eats incredible amounts of chocolate, pasta, and bread. Some athletes can focus too much on diet and develop disorders in which they binge or starve themselves, eating inconsistently. On our team we are not watched by the directors and doctors and we make our own food choices. Other teams have their doctors roving among the meal tables making sure the riders are only consuming foods that will keep them thin.

Victor Hugo Peña has a problem staying thin and not eating too much food. He loves meat, especially a thick steak, and will often eat a couple of steaks for dinner if they are good ones. He came from a team that completely controlled his diet. When the race was going slowly and the riders weren't exerting themselves, the director would call up the *soigneurs* in the feed zone and tell them to take food out of the bags. The riders had to check their weight daily, and if

> BENOIT JOACHIM HAS THE MOST SHOCKING DIET OF ANY OF THE RIDERS. HE CONSUMES A JAR OF NUTELLA IN A DAY OR TWO AT BREAKFAST AND ALSO EATS INCREDIBLE AMOUNTS OF CHOCOLATE, PASTA, AND BREAD.

they were heavier one morning they were told to eat less food. When Vic first joined U.S. Postal he gained a load of weight quickly because he overate—he wasn't accustomed to being in an environment where he had to monitor his own eating.

Victor is from Bucaramanga, Colombia. In 2001 I raced there at the Pan American Championships. I have never seen such huge crowds at a race. The entire 12-kilometer (7.5-mile) course was lined with spectators, and on the 2-kilometer climb the spectators were so dense there were only 2 meters of road for us to ride through.

In Colombia we had armed guards with us at all times to protect us from being kidnapped. The hotel was heavily guarded as well, but despite the presence of guns, the people were incredibly friendly and welcoming.

Along the roadside they sold Kool-Aid in plastic bags and fried ants in similar plastic bags. Two years after the Pan Am Championships, Victor arrived at the Vuelta with a bag of fried ants to share with all of us—a slightly crunchy pre-race snack loaded with protein.

CHAPTER SIX

RACING IN THE USA

Stepping off the plane in a daze and heading down the ramp to the passport checkpoint, it was easy to tell we were back in America. An armed guard stood at the gate as we got off of the plane. He held his hands on his hips, his stance wide. He had no smile but instead looked scornfully at the passengers walking off the plane.

Max said, "Man, coming to America now is like going to a present."

"A present?" I said.

"Yeah, a present. Look at these guys, they look at everybody like they're prisoners."

"Oh, a prison, you mean."

America has changed since September 11, 2001, and it is noticeable as soon as you get to the border. Nobody is smiling when you arrive, but instead airport staff is questioning travelers tersely. Signs are posted on the walls of what not to do. There is a feeling of guilt and fear that wafts through the stale air. It is an uncomfortable sensation that lifts slightly as soon as you step out into the fresh air.

The contrast between the United States and Europe became far more pronounced after living in Spain for much of the 2004 season. In the United States, people seem to be losing many of their freedoms due to the terrorist attacks on September 11, 2001, and the increased homeland security. I can understand the challenge Americans are now faced with after the attack on their country and feel sorry they have suffered from others' aggression.

The difference between American and European bike races and racers has also become more pronounced to me over the past few years. In America, there is always a sprint for the corner. Halfway through the race, riders dive underneath each other to gain a bike length. Bigger builds and muscle mass bulging from beneath the skin-suit top are used to intimidate. The riders are bigger in build as the races are shorter in length and flatter than in Europe but are fast and furious. Although the races are short, they require concentration. Letting off the pedals, or applying too much pressure to the brakes, places riders at the back. Riders don't pull in breakaways as they all have sprinters on their respective teams who can win. There is little respect for the profession and more respect for physical aggression.

As my team is an American team with an American title sponsor, it has had an obligation to race in the United States and to have a large percentage of American riders within the team. Each season we race the key events on the American calendar: the Redlands Classic and Sea Otter Classic in California, the Tour de Georgia, the three Wachovia races in and around Philadelphia, the New York City race,

Downer's Grove criterium national championships in Illinois, and the T-Mobile Grand Prix in San Francisco. For us it is nice to come back to the United States and race in an environment we know. As North American cyclists racing in Europe on U.S. Postal, we have a great advantage in the that we can come back home during the season, whereas those North Americans racing on foreign teams have less opportunity to return home, if at all, during the racing season.

In 2004 we had more American riders than in past years as the team makes a concerted effort to hire young Americans. When new riders are selected for the team, they are looked at carefully. Not only is it important that they have good results in bike races but also in physical laboratory testing. It is also necessary for a new rider to be able to fit into the team environment. There have been a few riders that have not fit the qualifications and they lasted on the team for short periods. The success of the team is a direct result of the riders that are hired. Individuals are not wanted but team members are desired.

✳

"*The air feels* good, polluted but good. We have been indoors or in planes for a day. Or how long has it been?" I asked, as Max and I stepped out of the terminal to meet the staff that was picking us up at the airport.

"I don't know, but I stink and feel sweaty all over," Max replied. "I have been looking forward to a good shower. Then we go out on the town, no?" he said with a smile, only half joking.

Max and I walked out of baggage claim and into the muggy, polluted airport parking. The smell of jet fuel and car exhaust, combined with the honks of drivers and the blast of the jets taking off, woke us out of our travel hangover.

Arriving at the hotel in Philly half an hour after the flight, we threw our gear in a room and walked to a local pizzeria down the block. The Lakers were on TV, the semifinals, and Julien DeVriese, our head mechanic, was entranced with the game as he cut into his pizza with a flexing plastic knife. The orange laminate tables, the lettered Pepsi menus above the cash register, it all felt like a place I knew. It felt good. Surreal though, as I was surrounded by a Flemish cycling crew that was glancing up at a Lakers game between bites of thick, cheesy pizza.

"Where yous guys from? Are yous here for that bike race?" asked the pizza parlor manager, hat turned backward, dressed in baggy jeans and basketball shoes.

"We're here for the race," responded Vince Gee, another mechanic.

"You like the Lakers?"

"I do," responded Julien, "and those bastards better win tonight."

"Are yous guys part of the team that that guy Lance Johnson rides for? You know, the guy that won the race in France?" the manager asked, as he got up from his seat in front of the TV to play with the air conditioner that was rigged precariously in the window with duct tape. After playing with the dials and switches for a few minutes, he left and opened the door to cool off the restaurant and then rejoined the conversation and the game.

"Yeah, that's us, U.S. Postal," responded Vince.

Julien loves coming to America for the races; they are, in fact, the only races where he works as a mechanic. Julien has been to more bike races than most of the riders combined, knows more about cycling than most of us, and has worked for Merckx, LeMond, and Lance as a mechanic. He is stubborn. The first year I raced with the team, I, along with most of the other riders, was scared of Julien. He would roll his eyes when I asked for a part to be changed or checked on the bike, making me feel as though I had asked for a new gold watch.

Julien rarely makes trips to the European races because he has done them all and because he keeps the team equipment in order at the warehouse and makes sure everything is running smoothly from the Belgian base. Julien comes to races in America because he loves America, the Lakers, and an afternoon ice cream.

Thirsty, and with no bottles, I went back to the team car during the 2003 Tour de Georgia for some water. Julien sat in the backseat, spare wheels beside him and a full cooler right behind the seat.

"What you want?" he barked as I rolled up beside the car.

"Bottles, please."

"The feed zone is coming up. Go back to the peloton."

I looked at him like he was kidding, and then realized he wasn't when he rolled up the window. "Prick!" I thought to myself. Why make me go all the way back to the peloton without bottles when they are right there, I am right there, and there are hours of racing to go?

That evening Laurenzo Lapage, our director in Georgia and the team's third director, came to my room. Laurenzo and Julien have known each other for ages and Laurenzo has a good understanding of Julien. He explained to me that Julien is a good guy, but he has ways of "playing with our balls," and that Julien got a kick out of it.

Laurenzo told me that he would joke with Julien in the car all day, playing tricks on him and nagging at him, but that Julien could also tell everything about a rider as soon as he saw him pedal—he could call a race from the backseat with one eye open while trying to sleep.

Julien apologized that night for not giving me water bottles, but only because the feed zone was much farther away than had been announced in the race manual, and we had to ride for an hour without water.

Julien has seen it all and had to deal with champions and assholes. He is extremely knowledgeable, and once you have proven yourself, he is also thoughtful. He doesn't believe in giving the riders more than they need but will also compliment you when you have raced well. And I now understand that when a compliment comes from Julien it has high value.

Philly is a great city and a city that embraces the USPRO Championships. The city seems to love the party that surrounds the race, or perhaps people turn the bike race into a party. The course is lined nearly the entire way around the 23-kilometer (14.4-mile) loop with spectators, and by the time the race nears its end at the six-hour mark, the course is packed with people 10 deep, the sidewalks jammed. The viewers are not all fans of cycling, but fans of the race in Philadelphia. The week prior to the event, shop fronts around town are decorated with bicycle displays celebrating the race.

Manayunk, a neighborhood in Philadelphia where all the action of the race takes place on the famous "Wall," has gone from being a rough and run-down neighborhood to a prosperous area lined with cafés, bike shops, galleries, and clothing boutiques, thanks in large part to the race. Each year tens of thousands of people fill the streets, eating hot dogs and hoagies while sipping beer and soda and encouraging us each time we pass.

The famous Manayunk Wall is lined with thousands of spectators, most drunk and ebullient with energy for the race. The fans are what help make the race the biggest event in American cycling. As a result of the fan base, the television coverage, its 20-year history, and the quality of the organization, it has become the premier event on the U.S. calendar that all of the U.S.–based professional teams make their goal for the season, and the race that all aspiring riders and veterans dream of winning.

Each morning, while back in the States, I got up early and stepped into the streets of Philadelphia. Cities come alive in the morning: the roadside carts, the skyscrapers splashing the cityscape with reflected sunshine, the aroma of eggs, bacon, and sausage filling the air, coffee to go, people hurrying to work, couriers running their first packages.

The race in Philly almost always unfolds in the same manner. A breakaway, sometimes quite a large one, gets established on the first ascension of the Wall. From there, the breakaway group will be given some rope off the front as the peloton rolls along at a comfortable speed. Once the gap gets large enough and teams start to worry about the break making it to the finish, the chase from behind begins. The break is caught in the final laps, the contenders on the Wall make vicious attacks, and the race for the victory unfolds.

Whenever the weather in Philly is cool, the race tends to be fast but not as hard. Hot temperature kills the field on the Manayunk Wall as one attack or effort zaps heaps of energy. The 2004 event was only 1 minute off the record, and we averaged 42.6 kilometers per hour (26.5 mph). Considering how slow the first hours of the race were, the last were certainly fast for us to get up to that average speed. Despite some very hard attacks in the final laps of the race and small breakaways coming from those attacks, the peloton still came into the last kilometer complete.

With four laps to go in Philly, the race unfolding and the peloton fast approaching the crucial final laps, a Saeco team rider, unhappy with the fact I was beside him in a corner, hit my handlebars hard when we hit the foot of the Wall in Manayunk. Without any time to react, I came crashing down onto the cobbled street. Adrenaline rushed through my body; I got back up immediately and raced up the climb toward the front of the peloton.

The race was going our way. The breakaway was under control and would be brought back, enabling us to set up the race for either a breakaway or a field sprint. I was to initiate or cover the attacks and Max was to sprint in the final.

The race finishes in front of the art museum in downtown Philadephia along the Schuylkill River. The European riders can be seen on the steps of the art museum taking photos of themselves in different Rocky poses, as those were the steps Sylvester Stallone ran up in his famous series of boxing movies. As I ride up and down the avenue of flags on Benjamin Franklin Parkway the week before the race in training, I get shivers down my spine. I can feel the history of the United States, the excitement of the race, and the intensity of the city. I feel alive.

The final meters of a race are chaotic. I was fully concentrated on the effort, on the peloton, on not crashing, on the job we needed to

CASEY B. GIBSON

PHILLY PACK: *The Postal team leads the peloton at the USPRO championships.*

get done. We had to get to the front with 1 kilometer to go, to get Max into position for the final sprint. With a couple of hundred meters to go, our job was done and it was up to Max to pedal with everything he had left to the line.

He didn't make it to the point where he could unleash everything he had left in his engine. I began accelerating, assuming he was on my wheel, with 500 meters to go. With 300, the sprint started to come around the head of the peloton that was breaking the wind. Max wasn't coming by me yet. With 200 meters, I let up on the pedals, a bad feeling coming over me since he hadn't gone by yet. The sprint was over and he hadn't sprinted.

Max had lost the race because his bike failed. Six hours of flawless racing and only seconds for it all to come undone. We left the race tired and frustrated.

Six hours in the saddle, racing through city streets, left us ready for a good meal and a relaxing evening. As the other riders sat in the lobby and nursed bottles of beer, the team showered and changed to catch the plane back to Europe. After a long race, brake dust and city grime is caked on our legs, faces, and arms. It is like paste and requires a good scrub to get off.

After a long race, my body feels odd: I am sweating profusely, I am tired but can't relax as my heart continues to thump hard and fast from the exertion of the race, my legs and arms ache, and I am constantly sipping at water to rid my mouth of dryness and to quench my insatiable thirst.

Five hours later the team was at the airport boarding a flight back to Europe. The racing was over and, like always, everyone was eager to get back home. In the airport we ate snacks and airport food for dinner. Max ate a burger while Benoit chewed on a dozen gumballs.

As Johan had said in the Algarve, "There is a race to the race, a race in the race, and a race to get home from the race."

The trip from Philly back to Europe is one of the only times that I travel home with Dede, as in Philadelphia both the men and women race on the same day, in different events. Sleeping on her shoulder while on the plane and opening the apartment door in Girona with her certainly takes away the loneliness we experience while on the road.

Since we met eight years ago in 1997, we have both raced there annually. Our families often travel to watch the races as well since it is their chance to see us both at the same venue.

The team races home from the events as quickly as possible because we all spend so much time away from home during the season. After Philly there is another race 10 days later, the Vuelta Cataluña in northern Spain, and we need to be recovered from jet lag and ready to race again.

It is not only important for the riders to get home quickly, but the staff must also prepare the trucks, bikes, and equipment for the upcoming races. The trucks need to be reloaded with bikes, spare wheels, and time trial bikes, as the team rosters are constantly changing and different riders are at the races requiring their own custom-fitted bikes.

We rarely travel with bikes to the races, only with our suitcases and backpacks. At home we have a training bike and at the races we have a race bike to race on and a spare bike that sits on the roof of the car in case of a mechanical problem. Our carry-on bags always carry our racing shoes, as baggage is often lost or delayed in transit. The one essential and unique piece of clothing for a cyclist is his shoes. Everything else, including the bikes, can be replaced and fitted, but shoes take a while to break in and adjust to. A misplaced cleat or an uncomfortable shoe can cause a knee injury that can ruin an entire racing season.

On the flight home Max talked about the race with Laurenzo the entire way as the rest of us fell in and out of sleep, wakened by the trolley as the food was served and disturbed by twitching and cramping in our legs due to muscle damage from the race and the lack of room between the seats. My stomach growled and its emptiness didn't allow me to get back to sleep until I ate a snack.

The plane landed in London and Max was still talking about the race. He had been talking about it for longer than the actual race lasted. Impressive. The next day we woke up and had another training ride to complete, another race to focus our thoughts on, and another chance at a victory in the coming week.

CHAPTER SEVEN

SUMMER IN SPAIN

*D*irk *received a call* from Luc. He was in the hospital without his wallet and would be late arriving at the race hotel in Spain.

When he arrived at breakfast, Luc looked like a team rider who had slid out on a tight mountain descent. He had road rash from head to toe, a swollen hand, and bandages all over his limbs.

Luc Verloo drives the bus throughout Europe from February until October. Before we drink our pre-race coffees, hold the race meeting, change into our chamois, and get to the start of the race, Luc often has to drive the bus through the night.

Driving a team vehicle in Europe has been a hassle for the staff ever since the 1998 "Festina Affair," in which the Festina team car was found with a pharmacy of banned performance-enhancing medicines during the Tour de France. Festina, a watch manufacturer that sponsored the team, ended its relationship with the sport in 2001. Since that Tour debacle, Luc, the mechanics, or the *soigneurs* will frequently be pulled over and have everything searched and their papers checked.

With less than 24 hours separating the finish of the Dauphiné Libéré in the French Alps and the start of the Vuelta a Cataluña, south of Barcelona, Luc drove nonstop in his typical and expeditious manner. His reward upon delivery of the team is sometimes as menial as a couple of hours of sleep before he resumes command of the driver's seat. Luc keeps a sleeping bag, a toothbrush, and some clothes in the bus so he has somewhere to sleep on the overnight trips when he can only afford a few hours of sleep. Notwithstanding his nomadic duties, Luc also has his bike tucked away in the belly of the bus and he'll sneak out when he can for a few hours on the road. He rides with us on the rest days, pointing out a "nice girl" along the coast or mixing it up with the boys for a town sign sprint.

After a long day of running around southern France in the team bus, Luc pulled over to take a short nap just outside Girona. He settled into a comfortable spot on the bus and shut his eyes.

Luc was enjoying his well-deserved rest in one of the comfortable leather seats when a shadow lurking in the bus startled him. As he jumped up he noticed the blue flash of an emergency light, intermittently illuminating the interior of the bus and the face of an intruder.

Luc jumped up and questioned what the intruder was doing on the bus. The man said he was with the police and demanded Luc's papers. Before Luc even had the time to pull his papers out, they were already in the man's grasp.

His heart now racing, Luc took off in pursuit of the intruder, who had blazed out the bus door. Without hesitating, Luc's adrenaline set him in pursuit of the intruder and the recovery of his wallet.

A small Euro hot rod of a car, blue siren still flashing, sat idling beside the bus, with its driver ready to hit the accelerator and take off. The man jumped in the car, and Luc lunged into the backseat. The car began to speed off, the smell of sweet air freshener thick in the air, the heavy notes of an Ibiza techno beat pounding out a rhythm in the night silence, and Luc's legs dragging on the pavement as he grasped at the car in hopes of getting his hands on the punk who was driving it.

Moments later he found himself back in the silence of the night, left with only the still odor of the countryside and the burn on his legs and his sandaled feet. He felt like he had just fallen from his bike at speed. The adrenaline release was gone and the pain from being thrown from the car was setting into his bones, his muscles, and his abrasions.

As he lay on the ground, his thoughts moved from losing his papers to how to get to the race in time for the start of the team time trial, how to get his wounds bandaged, and how to get some new papers.

The hotel room is hot and my legs are sweaty and covered in massage oil. A mosquito buzzes back and forth around my head. I flip the pillow for the cooler side and flip it again to find a more comfortable position. A scooter screams by the room and breaks the silence. I think of tomorrow and the season ahead. We are halfway through the season and nearing its heart. One more race and the team will be at the Tour de France.

The season can be broken up into three sections: the early season and spring classics; the Giro d'Italia and Tour de France; and then the fall classics, the Vuelta a España, world championships. There are riders who focus on one section or several, riders who look to one or two races, and riders who try to be consistent participants through most of the year. It is rare to see a rider who is victorious in the spring classics, competitive at the Tour, and then flying at the Vuelta and the world championships. In fact, not many riders have been able to do this since the 1980s.

The U.S. Postal team tended to focus mainly on the Tour, a little on the northern classics, and a little on the Vuelta. Come Tour time, there are usually 12 to 14 riders in good enough condition to do the race, whereas by the fall Vuelta, the team is usually easy to pick because there are fewer riders still going well due to the stress of the early season and the Tour. The season goes by quickly when I look back at it, but when I am in the middle of a stage race and suffering like a dog, it can sometimes seem really long.

The team had been flying in 2004, with perhaps its best spring ever. Max had been winning the field sprints; George had raced well in the northern races, as had Devolder; and Floyd had consistent results from the start of the year.

As I turn back and forth in bed, my mind climbs to the tops of the peaks we will ascend at the Vuelta a Cataluña and drives itself on the flats we rode in the team time trial earlier that day. The coastal breeze wafts through the window and a few crashing waves can be heard in the silence of the night air.

My mind keeps returning to the team time trial earlier that day. We lost, and we were beaten by a solid margin. My mom always told me not to look back and always look ahead, with no regrets and only lessons learned. But I keep thinking we should have gone faster. We had a good team for it and we were all motivated. There were a couple of minutes when we weren't at our limits and we lost 30 seconds. My thoughts keep reeling like a skipping record, coming back to the stretch of road, frustrating me and warming the cold side of the pillow. I force myself to think of Dede in Colorado, but I eventually end up back on the same stretch of road on the northeastern coast of Spain in Cataluña.

My thoughts then turn to the Tour. I was not selected for the 2004 Tour team. A few of the riders sleeping just down the hall will be on the team and a few others are in the running for the last spots. Everybody would like to go, but only nine will make the cut. I would love to be a part of the Tour team, but I try not to think too much about it. I toss and turn some more.

When selecting the team for the Tour, Johan and Dirk look for riders with experience, strength, and the individual qualities as a cyclist—whether the rider is a climber or a time trialist. The team needs to be made up of riders who are in peak condition in the month of July, who have either performed well at the Tour before or have experience in a grand tour, and most of all, riders who are selfless. It would be useless to have a team full of climbers or time trialists, so they select the riders to fill specific slots toward accomplishing the team's goals at the Tour. The team will need three or four climbers to accompany Lance in the mountains, and then three or four more powerful riders to protect him in the flatter terrain. I hope to make the Tour selection one day and yet I fully understand why I have yet to be selected. I don't have the experience or the fitness to set myself apart from the more experienced riders on the team.

The pressure within the team increases significantly as the Tour approaches—it is the key to our season. In 2003 the team had performed poorly throughout the spring, and as the Tour neared, the stress built up because our performance would make or break the season. We hadn't made any Union Cycliste Internationale (UCI) points, and if something had gone wrong in the Tour, the team would have been in rough shape in the standings that determine which races we are eligible for in the following season.

The 2004 season had been a lot more enjoyable thus far. When momentum gets rolling and we are winning races, the team ambiance is great. Everything flows more smoothly and the races even seem easier. The worst thing when you're a cyclist is to be nervous, to want the win too badly, because then you often either miss the objective fully or crash.

Summers in Spain are hot, hotter than anything I ever experienced back in the muggy Toronto summers. Our bike computers sometimes read 42 degrees Celsius (108°F) and hundreds of empty U.S. Postal bottles are tossed to the side of the road. In the early-season classics we go back to the car for water three or four times in a half day of racing, but in Spain we are constantly knocking on Dirk's window for more bottles.

Each year before the Tour, half of the team races in the Vuelta a Cataluña, a six-day race in Spain that starts on the Costa Brava, climbs through the Pyrénées, and finishes back down on the coast in Barcelona. For many of us, it is a highlight on the calendar because it is close to Girona and we can shower at home an hour after the last stage has finished.

In the 2004 Vuelta a Cataluña, Miguel Angel Martin Perdiguero of Saunier Duval dominated the first half of the week of racing, and in doing so locked himself in for the overall victory. He was known as a sprinter, but after a stellar week he could now be considered a time trialist and stage racer. Not only did he win the stage 2 uphill finish, but he also went on to win the mountaintop finish in Andorra with an explosive acceleration in the final meters, and the mountain time trial on the next day with the same explosive sprint over the last kilometer of the ascent.

Going into Cataluña, U.S. Postal didn't really have a leader to fill the role Roberto Heras had held for us in past years. Chechu was coming up in form but didn't know whether he had enough fitness to ride with the best on the big mountains. So we started with the attitude that we would race for stage wins. Max could win in a field sprint and the rest of us could try to win out of a breakaway.

The race started out with a team time trial (TTT) along the Mediterranean. It was a short race at 18 kilometers (11 miles) with lots of roundabouts and corners. Generally, TTTs tend to be straightforward on flat to rolling roads with few corners, and they are usually longer than 30 kilometers. We had a team that could have won the race because we had several TTT veterans and several young horses. The first half of the race didn't go our way; we never really found our rhythm. The second half we held even with the leaders—the Illes Balears team sponsored by Spain's Balearic Islands. But the time we lost in the first half did too much damage and we ended up with a depressing result.

The next few days of racing took us up to Andorra and the high mountains. It was a good trial for some of the Tour riders because they could test their legs on the longer climbs. Usually the riders who are going well in the Dauphiné and Cataluña are also competitive at the Tour de France since it starts only a few weeks later.

When we left the mountains and headed back toward the coast, we knew Max would have a chance at a stage victory. The courses were rolling to flat and could end in field sprints if we rode the race well and kept things under control in the last hour. The first shot we had at a victory was botched by misplaced signs that were intended to mark the final kilometers. In the last 10 kilometers (6.2 miles), the countdown to the finish is usually done by the kilometer once the finish line is within 5 kilometers. We didn't see the "5 kilometers to go" sign and only realized the finish was coming with 500 meters to go. And that was too late: the speed was so fast we couldn't move up more than 10 spots in that distance. The race organization had mistakenly placed the signs on another road that we didn't race on. We all finished a bit frustrated, hoping for a better result the next day.

All went according to plan on the penultimate stage. The team brought back the break and Max dominated the field in the hard uphill sprint finish. I don't think the other sprinters could even attempt to step off his wheel in the final meters. It is impressive to witness the power the sprinters can put out in a field sprint. They are hitting speeds upward of 60 kilometers per hour (37 mph) and are putting out over 1,500 watts.

The climbs in Andorra offered some picturesque views of the snowcapped peaks, and the valleys below along the coast were lush and green with life. One of the race stages that took us from the mountains toward the coast followed about 50 kilometers of road that we train on frequently while in Girona. It was nice knowing where we were going and what the profile of the course was during that section. It is not an advantage we can enjoy very often when racing in Europe.

Christian Vande Velde commented how weird it felt to be racing on one of his training roads—it seemed effortless in the peloton compared to when we were training.

During the race we were trying to cover the breakaways, Max not included. This position gives the team representation in the front, forces other teams to chase, and at the same time puts us in a position to win the stage. And, if it all comes together, the team rides on the front to help Max in the final sprint.

As always, the Tour de France team selections are made during the Cataluña race. While half of the team is racing in Cataluña, the riders who rode in the Dauphiné Libéré the week before are training in the Pyrénées. Since the Tour is the biggest race on the calendar and every rider on the team would love to race the Tour, there is competition within the team. With only nine spots available on the Tour team and about 13 riders racing well, the dynamic in Cataluña and the Dauphiné is odd; those two races are the only ones where that is true. All the riders who are in contention for the spots know that they need to perform in the races, and therefore they give it everything they have during the race, trying to outlast their teammates on the climbs or trying to pull extra hard while working on the front. Certain riders always try to get in front of the television motorbike as they know Dirk is watching the race on TV in the car and Johan from his

WITH ONLY NINE SPOTS AVAILABLE ON THE TOUR TEAM AND ABOUT 13 RIDERS RACING WELL, THE DYNAMIC IN CATALUÑA AND THE DAUPHINÉ IS ODD; THOSE TWO RACES ARE THE ONLY ONES WHERE THAT IS TRUE.

house. Halfway through the race, when the race reaches the high mountains, Johan shows up to follow in the car and gauge our fitness firsthand before making his final selection.

Once Cataluña is over, the riders who are not selected for the Tour de France team have a five-week break to rest, relax, and train for the second half of the season. For a few days, we can all be found lying on the beaches of the Costa Brava in the afternoons and then enjoying glasses of red Rioja wine with tapas in the evenings and ice cream for dessert.

Leading Up to July

BY GEORGE HINCAPIE

Riding on a team like U.S. Postal means winning a lot of races, a lot of the time. It means riding with some incredible teammates who do amazing things. I've spent a lot of time with my teammates, either training or racing, and, of course, sitting in the bus. Sitting there, exhausted, driving back to the hotel from races each day, you get to know your teammates in a way unlike in any other job in the world.

Riding with some of the best in the world means there are certain expectations; it means performing and succeeding under the toughest of pressure. In my career, I've done nine Tours de France, four Olympic Games, and several world championships. We've won races that have defined careers. It's been an incredible ride, but being part of a champion team means there are always challenges. To meet those challenges takes cohesion and a collective understanding of the team—something I've found hard to put into words. I have so many memories of waiting for a stage start in the bus, or leaving afterward, it's hard to choose any example that tells just what it's like to ride for the best cycling team in the world.

Take 2004's Dauphiné Libéré. The Dauphiné is a race in the French Alps that we do every June before the Tour de France. It's a warm-up for the Tour. An eight-day stage race in the French Alps, it has a couple of flat stages and a couple of mountain stages. One important reason we were at the Dauphiné in 2004 was to do the Mont Ventoux uphill time trial, which is an important test of one's Tour fitness. We arrived with relatively high expectations because our Tour team was strong, with the exception of one or two riders, and we were hoping to do well and gain confidence in this race before the Tour.

We certainly didn't expect to get our asses kicked, which we sort of did. Several teams were much stronger than we thought they would be. And although we knew we were not at 100 percent yet, we could only hope that the other teams were totally on top of their game. Teams like Euskaltel from Spain and Phonak from Switzerland rode much better than we expected.

So there was a lot of pressure on the team. We didn't have a sponsor for the next season. We had some negative press about Lance and the team. Somebody wrote a book about Lance that made false accusations. This was tough on the whole squad; you could feel it when we had dinner, when we sat in the bus, and when we were training. After the Dauphiné finished, we figured we really needed to buckle down and get our focus back for the Tour. We had the opportunity to win a record sixth-straight Tour de France.

The day after getting home from the Dauphiné, we packed up our stuff and rode our bikes six hours to a town in the Pyrénées called Puigcerdá. Since the town is in the mountains, it was no small task to get there by bike after riding over 1,002 kilometers (622 miles) in an eight-day stage race. We all knew what we had to do—hard work, and plenty of it—if we wanted to win the Tour. Our goal was to ride between five and seven hours a day, doing some reconnaissance of key mountain stages. We had terrible weather—6 degree Celsius temperatures (42°F) and pouring rain for the first few days. Being part of a team like ours means that rain or no rain, we still have to get out there and stick to the training as a team.

On the fourth day we went to ride one of the hardest stages of the Tour, finishing uphill to la Mongie. The idea was to do the climb a couple of times that day so we would know it for the Tour. As we crested it the first time, Lance and I discussed all the negative press and the off-putting things people were saying about him and the team. With each pedal stroke, we both got really upset—it was having a terrible effect on us mentally. But halfway up the climb, we rounded the corner and on the left there was a big run-down shack. On this shack was written, in English, "Anger is a Gift!" It was incredible; it felt like an omen. Lance and I just stared at it in utter disbelief. We had goose bumps all over.

It was almost fate. Just as we thought we were losing our focus, we saw the shack and the saying, and we both looked at each other and said, "We need to get it together!" We both felt the endorphins, the energy, the anger, flow through us, and our legs came alive.

We trained hard that day, and the next, and the next. And when we got to France a few weeks later, we raced as a team that was inspired to win. And we did—our record sixth Tour.

Our commitment to excellence is exactly what led us to that primitive shack in the Pyrénées after the Dauphiné Libéré this spring. It's the same feeling that buzzes in the bus before the stages; it's magical being a part of it.

CHAPTER EIGHT

THE 2004 TOUR DE FRANCE

*T*he first Tour de France was organized in the summer of
1903 by Henri Desgrange as a publicity stunt for his sporting
newspaper *L'Auto*. There had been many bike races before 1903, but
all had been one-day or single-stage events. The Tour de France was
to be the first multistage race and would take the riders around the
entire "hexagon" of France.

For the first Tour, there were 6 stages over 19 days, averaging 404
kilometers (252 miles) in length, for a total of 2,428 kilometers (1,508
miles). The winner, Maurice Garin of France, completed the course at
an average speed of 25.6 kilometers per hour (16 mph), a remarkable
feat considering the terrain, the bikes, and the condition of the roads
in those days. Some stages took more than 18 hours to complete.

The first Tour was a great success, gleaning publicity and sales for
L'Auto. The success of the first Tour, however, and the passions it gen-
erated among the sporting public were almost its downfall. The 1904
Tour was marred by cheating, with riders taking shortcuts and hitching

lifts in vehicles and trains. The fans were the biggest problem, hurling abuse and threats at their rivals and scattering tacks in the road so that riders would puncture tires. The final results for that race were not announced until the following December, when it was revealed that four of the leading riders had been disqualified. Maurice Garin, who again had the best time, was one of those disqualified, and the final win went to Henri Cornet of France.

The publicity gained by *L'Auto* was matched by the publicity gained by the manufacturers of the bicycles ridden by leading riders. By 1913 the Tour had grown to 15 stages and 5,387 total kilometers (3,347 miles). The average stage was still 360 kilometers (223 miles) and the longest 470 kilometers (291 miles). Compare this with a modern Tour of around 3,500 total kilometers (2,170 miles) over 20 days and an average stage of 175 kilometers (109 miles).

> BY 1913 THE TOUR HAD GROWN TO 15 STAGES AND 5,387 TOTAL KILOMETERS (3,347 MILES).... COMPARE THIS WITH A MODERN TOUR OF AROUND 3,500 TOTAL KILOMETERS (2,170 MILES) OVER 20 DAYS.

The Tour is a great test of rider and machine, and the bike manufacturers proudly advertise their product's reliability. There were no spare bikes available for the riders in the early Tours. Race regulations stated that the rider himself must complete all repairs. In 1913, race leader Eugene Christophe was descending the Tourmalet Pass in the Pyrénées when his front fork broke. He had to run several kilometers with his bike on his shoulder to a blacksmith's forge in Ste. Marie de Campan. There he repaired the fork while race officials stood over him to ensure that the rider alone completed the work. The time lost cost

Christophe the race, but the officials still penalized him 3 additional minutes because the blacksmith's apprentice assisted by pumping the bellows to the forge.

There was no Tour between 1915 and 1918, the first of two breaks due to the World Wars. Apart from those periods, the Tour has been held every year, celebrating its one hundredth anniversary and its ninetieth edition in 2003.

The spectacular performances of the early Tour riders are even more impressive when one considers that the bikes they rode had no gear mechanisms. The bikes were equipped with sprockets on either side of the rear wheel. When the rider needed to change gears, he had to stop, remove the rear wheel, and turn it around so that a different sprocket could be used. Even though touring bicycles had derailleurs before 1930, the Tour organizers would not allow their use until 1936. Surprisingly the use of derailleurs made little difference to the average speed of the winner. Speed increased by less than 1 kilometer per hour.

The belief that the riders should be self-sufficient persisted until the 1950s. Only then was a rider permitted to change a complete wheel in case of a puncture. Prior to that, riders were required to carry spare tires and a pump and change the tire themselves. A complete wheel change was only allowed if the wheel itself was damaged.

Tour de France riders come in all sizes. The small, light riders have an advantage when the road goes up, but the heavier, more robust riders have the advantage in the tough conditions on the flat. Jean Robic was a small, light rider who excelled in the mountains but found his lack of weight to be a handicap on the descents. To overcome this disadvantage he was known to pick up a lead-filled bottle at the top of a mountain pass.

The time difference between the first- and second-place riders in the Tour varies tremendously. The time gap between Maurice Garin and second-place Lucien Pothier in 1903 was 2 hour, 49 minutes. In 1989 Greg LeMond won by just 8 seconds over Laurent Fignon, and most modern Tours are won by a time gap of less than 10 minutes. Modern-era riders are far better trained than their predecessors and more closely matched in ability. New bicycle technology, better roads, and superb team support all add up to very fast speeds. The modern Tour is won at around 40 kilometers per hour (25 mph).

Today at the end of a race, the rider's every need is taken care of by his team and the race organization. That wasn't the case for many of the riders in the early Tours. The top riders even then were professionals and were looked after by their team officials, but there were amateur riders, known as *touristes-routiers*, who competed unassisted. For them there were no accommodations arranged at the stage finish and no meals provided. After finishing a daunting 450 kilometers, they were expected to find their own accommodations. To help pay for room and meals, many were reduced to begging in the streets.

One of the attractions for the fans at the start of a Tour stage is the signing-on ceremony. Every rider is required to write his name on the sign-in sheet and is presented to the crowd. The present-day sign-on is purely ceremonial, but in the early days riders were not only required to sign at the start but at controls along the route and at the finish. This ensured that they had at least completed the course. It didn't, of course, ensure that they hadn't hitched a lift between controls.

The month of July is the focus of the U.S. Postal team's entire racing season. For the nine riders selected for the Tour team, that is their focus. Meanwhile, the rest of us take a break from racing and begin training for the late summer and early fall races. With six weeks at home in Girona to train and focus on the 2004 Olympic Games and the Vuelta, I was able to watch the Tour on television each day, following the team's effort to win for the sixth time in a row.

Each morning I would wake up to the sticky summer Spanish air, eat breakfast, and climb on my bike for a training session. I made sure I was always home in time to catch the last hour of the Tour. Although I arrived home from training drained from the effort in the intense heat, I would be glued to the TV, while lying on the couch, dripping with sweat, wearing only my boxer shorts.

Watching races for an athlete is difficult because there is an ever-present desire to compete and to be there. I don't watch too many cycling races on television when my teammates are not racing, but having trained and raced with Postal's Tour team I had to watch the race play out.

Lance rolled down the start ramp in pursuit of his sixth consecutive Tour de France victory. No cyclist in the race's 100-year history had achieved such a goal. In a race that Lance had dominated for the past five years, he started 2004 as the clear favorite.

The team that was formed around Lance was the strongest unit in the race. There were riders within the team with the ability to race for stage victories or a top place in the final overall classification, but they

Chitty Chitty Bang Bus

BY CHRISTIAN VANDE VELDE

Come July, the U.S. Postal team is a force to be reckoned with—a highly structured team that has dominated cycling in recent years. It is a huge team that always manages to come up diamonds, even when the chips are down. But not too many people remember back to the 1990s when the team was just getting its footing in France.

Most people are familiar with the sight of the U.S. Postal team driving into a race parking lot. A few team cars, an unmarked team car, maybe a small van, and the huge bus with the U.S. Postal Service logo painted all over it. But back in 1998, we had just one camper. And I don't mean a plush camper like you see all the snowbirds driving in on their way down to Arizona. This was a Euro camper: no AC and tiny "bedrooms." In fact, I remember Anton Villatoro being scolded by Julien DeVriese after he had a bowel movement in the van before the Tour of Flanders. Anton had the valid argument, asking why we had a bathroom if we couldn't use it? But, somehow, the bathroom was off-limits to Anton, and since we were actually renting the camper from Julien, his word was the law.

By 1999 we had two campers! We were pimpin'. But even with two campers that didn't mean we were any more comfortable. Lance, Tyler, and Kevin Livingston were in one, so that meant six other guys had to find a seat in the other. We all staked our claim to different seats, and poor Jonathan Vaughters was relegated to the team car. To be honest we really didn't have that much room for each rider, so often I just laid on the floor—a habit I can't seem to break no matter how big our bus is now. We rolled into the first stage of the 1999 Tour de France with the yellow jersey, team classification, and two "badass" campers. We were suddenly stricken with the realization of what we had on our hands.

Driving in the camper we were still the underdogs and we looked like it. Lance wasn't expected to win the Tour that year and we weren't expected to be capable of supporting him. We just took it day by day, sweating our butts off in that camper on the way to the hotel and to the race, with me lying on the floor because it was just too hot to sit close to one another.

About halfway through the race, we nicknamed a woman who we saw each day as "Chocolate Mary," because she gave us over 20 pounds of chocolate turtles throughout the race. She was a friend of Frankie Andreu and George Hincapie, and she had always pushed her homemade chocolates on them. We would stuff them into our little fridge and they became a new fixture of post-race nutrition. They made our guts virtually sick, day after day, but we loved indulging in these rewards after a hard day's work.

I am also sure of the fact that if Manolo, my director at Liberty Seguros during 2004, saw one of his boys consuming a chocolate turtle washed down with coke after six hours of suffering, there would be words and maybe even the sounds of your bike coming out from the storage bay under the bus so that you could ride your hypoglycemic ass home. But hey, that was then, and this is now. ❈

dedicated all of their energy to helping Lance get to Paris in the yellow jersey at the end of July. The most important factor in selecting the Tour team is that each member has a sole objective: help Lance win the Tour. Nobody has personal ambitions, and the mentality is all for one.

The Tour de France organization unveils the course for the race nearly nine months prior to the start of the event. Towns pay the race organization for starts and finishes, because the Tour coming to a town brings international recognition and draws countless tourists. The day of the race becomes a summer festival that all of the towns-people mark on their calendars months before the event.

When Lance and Johan look at the course for the upcoming year, they develop a plan that details Lance's training months prior to the race and which races he will undertake to prepare himself physically and mentally for the Tour. In 2004, the course was perhaps one of the most challenging ever—many experts said it was designed to break Lance's winning streak and deny his attempt at a record sixth victory.

At training camp in January, plans were already being made for the Tour in July, and preliminary plans had also been formed at the team's first training camp in Austin in December. Races leading up to the Tour are selected if they have qualities that mimic the stages the team will encounter in the Tour. The team will enter races that have individual time trials, mountain time trials, and hard climbs in order to hone the team's skills prior to the Tour start. This tactic has been used each year since Lance's first Tour victory. The team approaches the race with similar tactics each year as well.

Not only is the Tour de France the hardest, most physically demanding sporting event of the year, but it is also a tactical game in which riders are selected to sacrifice themselves for their leader.

Strategies are devised months in advance and are executed with the fervor of a battalion going into the field of combat. Johan Bruyneel and Dirk Demol build the team with every tactical circumstance in mind as well as the course the Tour covers. There was to be no weakness within the team they selected.

Each Tour team is made up of nine riders. U.S. Postal has formed a well-rounded team around Lance, as he needs support in both the mountains and on the flat roads. The one role that the team has consistently placed less emphasis on is that of a sprinter. This is because the team isn't really interested in winning the flatter stages. To win the overall, all of the riders' energy has to be focused on the sole objective of getting Lance the yellow jersey in Paris. In French, the language of cycling, Lance's teammates, his helpers, are called *domestiques*.

These riders are essentially in the race to ride in the wind and pull on the front for Lance, to get him bottles and keep him well fueled during the races, and to set the race up tactically so he can ride toward victory. For Lance, it is important to remain sheltered from the wind and conserve energy for the critical points in the race. When drafting behind his teammates in this way, he is doing 20 percent less work. Over a three-week race, consistently doing 20 percent less work saves energy for the big attacks.

The team is key to Lance's success. Certain riders are selected for the Tour to help Lance in the first week of the race, where it will be crucial to keep him well positioned near the front of the peloton and out of the wind. It is always important that Lance makes it through the first week without crashing or having expended too much energy. The third and final week of the race is often the hardest. Therefore, it is key that Lance enters the last week as fresh as possible.

In the first week of the race in 2004, George Hincapie, Viatcheslav Ekimov, Pavel Padrnos, and Benjamin Noval were on the front often keeping Lance and the other climbers, José Azevedo, Triki Beltran, and Chechu Rubiera out of the wind and in key positions. Floyd Landis is a versatile rider and works on the flats or rides a hard tempo in the mountains. In 2004, he was saved for later stages when the race hit the Pyrénées and the Alps.

The team has an incredible amount of experience and most of the riders have carried Lance to victories in the Tour in the past. The only riders who were new to Postal's Tour team were José and Benjamin. José has ridden for Joseba Beloki, one of Lance's rivals in past Tours, and he has personally placed well in three-week tours. Benjamin is a big horse of a rider—a quiet, nice Spaniard from Asturias—with great power to help the team keep things under control on the flats and over the smaller climbs.

The U.S. Postal team lineup is formed with the sole purpose of getting Lance to Paris in yellow, but not all the teams in the Tour de France are racing for the overall victory. Realizing that only a handful of riders in the professional peloton are capable of attaining such a goal, other teams aim at other objectives in the race, such as winning stages, going for one of the other jerseys, or trying to place one of their riders in the top 10 of the overall classification. Since cyclists are rolling billboards for their sponsors, the organizations that run the teams are always content when they have riders in breakaways getting television coverage with their sponsors' logos across the screen for hours at a time.

For instance, during the three weeks of racing, some riders often go in breakaways that don't have much chance of making it to the finish because they never get much of a gap on the peloton or are simply left to hang out front by the powerful peloton that looms behind. Yet, the riders in the breakaway continue to pedal like mad to stay out front for as long as possible—the cameras are on their jerseys, their names are plastered on the television screens, and all the newspapers discuss their efforts off the front of the peloton the next morning.

Many of the stages take as long as a trans-Atlantic flight, with the riders consuming thousands of calories and several liters of water in one stage. Riders push on and keep pedaling despite cuts from crashes, cramps in their legs, and days more to go. Only when their injuries are so bad that they can no longer pedal will they stop and return home, usually in tears.

The first week of the 2004 Tour was the most dangerous: the peloton of riders was nervous passing over cobbles and encountered wet, windy, slippery conditions. The riders racing for the general classification typically want to ensure that they don't lose time needlessly on the flatter stages, where the greatest dangers are crashes and strong winds that can splinter the peloton. Positioning in the wind is key and this is where team leaders such as Lance rely on their teammates to keep them out of the wind but still close to the front. A rider at the back can lose minutes or more on a windy stage just because he is poorly positioned.

The 2004 Tour route included a few challenges that Lance and the team hadn't faced in past years: the cobbles in the first week, the onslaught of mountain stages in the final two weeks, and a time trial up the steep and sinuous alpine pass, l'Alpe d'Huez.

The organizers made the last week incredibly intense, which threw another curveball at Lance and the team, as they had never been faced with two time trials in the last days of racing. Lance and the team went over every inch of the roadway for the last two time trials and most of the mountain stages in preparation for what was to come.

Preparation of the equipment to be used in the Tour de France is also a yearlong project. The carbon Trek bicycles are designed to be the fastest and lightest possible, using the most advanced technology. With partners like AMD and Trek, the team starts the Tour with the best bikes available for the task at hand. AMD processors have helped in the development of the riders' equipment, from clothing to helmets to bikes, an advantage that helps keep them in front and trouble free during the races.

In training prior to the Tour, many of the riders on the U.S. Postal team use power meters. The power meter has become the standard training tool for much of the peloton in the past five years. It is a small computer, mounted on the handlebars, that can track the rider's performance. The computer will give readings on wattage, speed, distance, heart rate, cadence, and kilojoules (the caloric expenditure during the workout). After a training session, we can download the workouts into our computers and send the data to our coaches. Whether the coach is down the street or in another country, he can see exactly what we have done for training that day by viewing the file on his computer.

Using the power meter and the laptop, we can also simulate the race while training. With the distance, time, and watts, we can parallel a race effort. In the weeks prior to the Tour, Lance and the team trained in the mountains with their power meters. During these sessions Lance could use this tool to gauge his fitness and to determine whether he was ready to take on the mountains and his competitors.

For the 2004 season, it was mandated that we were no longer allowed to race with the old-style nonprotective time-trial helmets. Instead, we were to use only approved helmets that met the regulations required for road races. The helmet manufacturers raced to produce a legal helmet. For the Dauphiné Libéré and the Giro d'Italia, they came out with a sleek helmet

RIDING THE COBBLES: *Hincapie pushes the pace at the '04 Tour de France.*

that could also save a rider's head in case of a crash. Prior to the Dauphiné, we were racing in time trials with our Giro road helmets covered in plastic to make them more aerodynamic.

Lance has taken over from where Greg LeMond left off when it comes to technology and finding the most aerodynamic equipment. In addition to being aware of the importance of sponsorship and marketing in cycling, they both are keenly aware of the importance of keeping up with technology.

Greg LeMond brought the baseball cap into the European peloton in the late 1980s. On the final podium of the 1989 Tour de France, he wore a pink fluorescent Coors Light baseball hat, and the European press went crazy over his wearing an American trucker's hat on the Champs-Elysées. But the hat was the ideal billboard for the sponsor and was seen the following day on newsstands across the world. A year later many riders were stepping up onto the podium with baseball hats, their sponsors' name plastered across the front.

LeMond also changed cycling in another more important dimension when he won the '89 Tour. He stormed up the Champs-Elysées on a bike with outstretched handlebars that put him into a position like a downhill skier in a tuck. He was laughed at when he rolled out of the start gate, but when it was later proven in the wind tunnel that it was the handlebars that had won him the Tour de France, every team adopted them. They have been an essential piece of equipment for almost any race against the clock ever since.

In 2003 a skinsuit was developed by Nike for Lance and U.S. Postal that is much more aerodynamic; it hugs the skin tight, has a rough feel to the fabric much like the dimpled surface of a golf ball, and has few seams, zippers, or elastics that would increase drag. At the Athens Olympics the same technology was used throughout the Games by many of the time trialists and also by athletes in track and field events. At our early-season training camps, Nike designers measured the riders for the skinsuit, and then took photos of them in the suits on their time-trial bikes to document how the fabric fitted to the body.

Before the Tour, all the guys packed up their gear and flew to Liège, Belgium. In the days prior to the start, they underwent medical testing and they did a few training rides on their time trial bikes in preparation for the prologue and team time trial. Most of the training in the week prior to the start is easy, because all the hard work in preparation for the Tour has already been done. Rest, relaxation, massage, and a good diet are the most important in the days before the Tour begins.

The medical tests determine whether the riders are healthy enough to race. These are not only blood tests, but also physical exams. They check Lance's body fat, weight, resting heart rate, and blood pressure in front of dozens of photographers and media. Christian Vande Velde told me that it was one of the most embarrassing moments of his career. There are plenty of photos of Lance with his shirt off, Oreo tan lines and ribs poking out, floating about in the media.

During the season, professional cyclists submit blood tests to the UCI on a quarterly basis so that the governing body can follow trends in the blood for signs of doping and also to check whether a rider is healthy. The tests have proven useful for health tests as well as doping regulatory tests. I know riders who have discovered health problems that would have most likely gone unnoticed if they hadn't gone through the blood tests.

The week prior to the Tour is perhaps the longest of the season for the riders. All the hard work has been done, they are ready to go, and they sit in their hotel rooms eager to get it all under way and race down the starting ramp. The world waits eagerly for the fight for yellow to begin.

A bit of sad news came in before the start of the Tour. Matt White, who was now racing with Cofidis, crashed while previewing the prologue course in the morning and wasn't able to start the race. Whitey had dreamed of racing in the Tour since he began cycling, and he was set to start his first in 2004. I saw him a few days earlier and you could see the excitement in his eyes and hear it in his voice. He is a great guy and I think everybody in the Tour peloton wanted him to be there.

The prologue time trial, much like the prologue in a book, is intended to introduce the Tour de France, the storyline, its peloton of riders, its champions, its characters and protagonists to the public. The prologue was only introduced to the race in 1967, and it has become a great tool for the commentators and press to introduce the riders to their audience. After the Tour adopted the prologue, virtually every other stage race began to include a prologue in its program.

The prologue is a short effort in which little time is won or lost. Lance goes into the prologue with the same focus as for a longer time trial—he wants to gain as much time as possible on any skinny mountain-goat climbers who may give him a hard time in the Pyrénées and the Alps. In the Tour every second counts, as Lance learned in 2003 when his 61-second margin of victory was the smallest of all his Tour victories.

> THE PROLOGUE WAS INTRODUCED TO THE RACE IN 1967, AND IT HAS BECOME A GREAT TOOL FOR THE COMMENTATORS AND PRESS TO INTRODUCE THE RIDERS TO THEIR AUDIENCE.

The prologue is also important because it sets the tone for the race. A strong ride will strike fear into the other competitors. It is important that Lance and the rest of the team ride well in this first effort, because the team's start position in the team time trial that follows will be determined by the team's position in team classification, which is calculated with the times of the team's top three finishers in each stage. They want to be the last to start the team time trial so they can have all the time references to the other teams ahead.

The riders race the prologue on time trial bikes, fully kitted-out in aerodynamic helmets, special clothing, and special wheels. In the last 15 years aerodynamics and weight have become key factors in bike racing. It is amazing to feel the difference in speed between the lower-profile time trial bike and the standard road bike. For the same wattage output, speeds are much quicker on a time trial bike. But a time trial bike is not as comfortable on longer rides and not as versatile—you can't climb efficiently on a time trial bike, or negotiate corners or descents quite as well. The bikes look much different. The Spanish riders call the time trial bike their *cabra*, or goat, because of their hornlike handlebars

In all of the Tour's time trials, one of the team's riders ranked lower on the classification, usually a rider who is a good time trialist, goes as hard as possible over the first half of the course—and if he is feeling good, over the entire route—to establish time references for Lance, who will race later. For example, Ekimov, the 2000 Olympic time trial champion, started early in the prologue and set the standard for Lance. During the time trial, Johan follows riders in the team car and gets time checks on the course so they can gauge Lance's ride later in the day. All the riders wear radios so their intermediate times can be communicated to them during their time trial. Lance chose to start the prologue in his USPS team kit instead of his 2003 yellow jersey because he wanted to first "earn" the yellow jersey in 2004.

Lance set the stage for a great Tour when he left the start house in Liège. He looked smooth and powerful, accelerating hard out of the corners while always maintaining his speed and a high cadence. He managed to gain time on his rivals as well, putting both his teammates and himself in a good position as they rode into a stressful first week on the flatter roads of Belgium and northern France.

Racing the Tour de France takes up the cyclists' whole day, every day, for 21 days of racing and two rest days. The races last between four and seven hours, but the days and evenings are filled with eating, preparing for the race, racing, recovering from the race, and then preparing for the next race day.

The Tour is a traveling caravan and the riders see little outside of it during the race. They may catch an hour or two of CNN or the local news in the evening, but aside from that the world outside the race is indeed a world away.

The stages usually start in the late morning or early afternoon, so riders either sleep in and have one big breakfast three hours before the race, or get up earlier and eat two smaller meals. Floyd, for example, wakes up before everybody else, often before the staff, so he is at the breakfast table drinking coffee alone while the others are still in bed. Chechu, on the other hand, is a true Spaniard and sleeps until the very last minute, which is usually when one of the staff pounds on the door to wake him up.

Each night before bed, Johan or Dirk bring an itinerary to each rider's room that outlines what's on tap for the next day. The schedule has a time for breakfast and pasta (which is basically a second break-fast or early lunch), a time for the suitcases to be ready (they are packed in the truck and brought to the next hotel before the riders arrive), a time to leave for the race, where the day's race tactics meeting will be held prior to the race, the time the race starts, the distance, and how far the next hotel is from the finish. With the schedule, the rider has no excuse for not being informed or on time. Invariably, though, someone is late or asks when we're leaving or how we're getting to the hotel after the finish.

When the hotel is close to the start line, that's a luxury for the staff and riders since the transfer time is minimal. Then there's more time to relax and get ready for the race in the hotel rather than sitting in the team bus on the way to the start. Regardless of whether there's a long or short transfer, the team meetings are always held in the bus an hour before the race. The riders sip on espressos from the bus's coffee machine while Johan goes through the day's course and race plan. I chatted with George the morning of stage 2 as he was getting ready to race, and he said he was looking forward to getting through the first few days. The nerves in the peloton were high during the early stages of the race. Although those stages weren't incredibly hard physically, they were mentally draining on the riders because they had to be constantly on the alert for attacks, wind, obstacles in the road such as roundabouts or traffic islands, and crashes.

During several of the flatter stages there were crashes on the wet, slippery roads. The "Spanish Mafia," as the three Spaniards on the team—Chechu, Triki, and Benjamin—have been affectionately nicknamed, all crashed at the same moment, in the same section, and were all bandaged the following day.

The team is prepared for every scenario and is always ready for an injury, whether it is from overuse and stress on a muscle or joint or the result of a crash. Two doctors travel with the team during the Tour, as well as a chiropractor and the four *soigneurs*. To heal an injury staff use everything from lasers to special tape that is elastic and fluorescent in color. The tape pulls the muscle away from the stressed tendon, letting it rest so it can heal quicker. In the bus there are also ice packs ready to be applied. At races several riders will have packs on their knees, necks, or backs.

We all also pack tension socks in our suitcases. Worn during travel days and after races, the socks, either knee-high or full-length, look much like women's nylons and increase blood flow while also limiting swelling that occurs during long travel at altitude where we're motionless and cramped in a plane seat. The socks were initially tested on the bike and were to be used by the team in time trials, but the UCI halted their use since they do not conform to the UCI's fashion regulations. The tension socks have become widely used in track and field. They are definitely a benefit when we travel because our legs are less bloated when we get off the plane and it is much easier to get on the bike and ride.

For most of the peloton in 2004, the serious stress during the Tour began when the course passed over a few sectors of the famous cobbles of the Paris-Roubaix race. Our team had planned for it and was ready for battle. Lance and Johan knew this would be a decisive day in which riders could be eliminated from the battle for the yellow jersey due to misfortune or disorganization within the team.

Riding on cobblestones is similar to having the dentist's drill in your mouth: you feel every vibration throughout your whole body, which tenses up, so you cannot find any position of comfort. The only relief comes when it has all ended and every muscle and tendon in your body can relax.

Racing on the cobbles is not only physically stressful for the riders but also mentally stressful. The U.S. Postal team faired extremely well and protected Lance, keeping him at the front of the race through all of the dangerous sections. The only really low point for the team was when Benjamin Noval crashed. He seemed to come out of it all right and managed to get back up and keep pushing to the finish line.

Asturias, where Benjamin lives, is a province in northwestern Spain on the Atlantic. Benjamin lives close to Chechu and often trains with him. Benjamin's father owns a bar-restaurant in Asturias, and in the off-season Benjamin can be found pouring Asturian apple cider behind the bar or serving up meals to the clients.

Benjamin came to our team in 2004 from a smaller Spanish team after having a great season in 2003. He arrived at U.S. Postal not knowing much English. Halfway through the spring he was able to talk with us in English. By the end of the year he could understand much of what was said.

As expected, it was not the difficulty of the cobbles that split the field and caused the major pileups; it was the nervousness of the peloton in the lead up to the first cobbled section that caused trouble. The biggest crash of the day happened when Iban Mayo, one of Lance's main rivals for the overall, went down.

The cobbled section and the crashes eliminated a couple of the contenders for the overall victory, as was predicted. Both Mayo and his teammate Haimar Zubeldia, two riders who found themselves in the hunt for the yellow jersey in 2003, finished the day over 4 minutes behind Lance. I think Lance would be the first to say that this isn't the way he likes to gain time on his adversaries. At the same time, bike racing is not only about going up the mountains fast but also about steering clear of crashes and regaining momentum after flat tires and mishaps. It was, however, unfortunate and a bit heartbreaking to see Mayo watch the race roll away in front of him.

I know many of our Postal riders were quite worried about crashes in the lead up to—and on—the cobbled sections. However, because most of the team had seen the sections before, they had a good idea of what to expect. They knew where and when they needed to be well positioned in the bunch. George and Eki were Lance's wingmen, keeping him in front and out of trouble. Both riders are cobblestone veterans and love a good battle on the Roman roads. Lance couldn't have had two better guys.

One of the highlights of the Tour, from the TV-watcher's perspective, was when George and Eki were hammering away on the front of the peloton, over the cobblestones, a trail of dust behind them, and Lance's Texas-starred helmet poking out occasionally from the group behind. The two of them made it look easy. To hit the cobbles as a trio is extremely difficult since the entire peloton wants to do the same. Then to drive it the way they did, in total dominance, for the entire sector was awesome. I am sure Johan was yelling in their earpieces the entire time, even though they couldn't hear him since the crowds, motorcycles, and helicopters above created overpowering background noise. It was definitely exciting to see a Tour stage on the cobbles.

CHAPTER NINE

THE TEAM TIME TRIAL

The team time trial was another high-pressure day for U.S. Postal. Everyone on the team had to be fully concentrated and tapping his limit physically for the entire race. The team was aiming to gain more time on its adversaries and also go for the stage win.

In the team time trial everybody has to be in sync. A strong but stupid rider can do more damage to a team than a weak rider sitting on the back. Ideally the team rides as a unit, each taking turns at pulling on the front. The key to racing a good team time trial is having smooth flow in which every rider is pulling at the same speed. Hard accelerations at the front of the team hurt everyone following behind, and therefore the stronger riders don't pull faster but longer. They may increase the speed of the team but they do so progressively to avoid breaking the rhythm. Riding a steady, fast TTT is an art, and our team has perfected it. Being a member of a fast team, a winning team, in a team time trial is one of the most fulfilling experiences for a cyclist.

The time trial events during a stage race may seem a lot shorter than the other stages in distance and time, but the days actually end up being quite a bit longer. On the day of the TTT, the team typically rides once in the morning after breakfast and then again in the race in the afternoon. The morning ride is simply to open up the legs and body, basically a warm-up. After the morning ride of about 50 kilometers (31 miles), the riders have a lunch of pasta or rice and an omelet. Prior to the time trials they eat foods that are easy to digest and they also make sure to eat three hours before the race to ensure that they aren't burping up their lunch during the race.

Before a time trial it is important to get warmed up because the effort is quite vicious—the riders' heart rate will average between 170 and 190 beats per minute for the entire event. Generally, everyone on the team will line up outside the team bus and ride their time trial bikes on the stationary trainers. They progressively increase their tempo over an hour and then do a few hard efforts toward the end of the warm-up.

It is awesome to see the entire team lined up outside the bus, sweating like crazy, heads bopping to music blasting out of their iPods, with eyes completely focused ahead, lost in their work. In 2002 we all used Discmans, or minidisc players, and now almost the entire team is plugged into iPods. Music preferences differ throughout the group, from hip-hop to Spanish pop to European techno.

As the different teams prepared themselves on the start line at the Tour TTT, I could tell which ones were motivated to achieve a good ride and which ones were dreading the event. Our team was incredibly focused. Everybody on the team looked ahead, eyes focused, with none of the circus around the start line causing any distraction. It is this focus that wins bike races.

George's Team Time Trial

BY GEORGE HINCAPIE

I remember driving to the team time trial at the Tour one year, getting off the bus and feeling a bit nervous the first time we did it—it was a very intimidating experience for me. The team time trial is a very high-speed event, with nine men riding together to go as fast as they can. There's really no margin for error—I guess that's what makes it so stressful. We ride at 50 to 65 kilometers per hour (30 to 40 mph) just inches from each other for an hour or more.

The 2004 TTT was held on a horrible day. It was pouring rain. Several teams had crashed before we even started, and we knew the course was dangerous. We knew how much time we could lose and still be safe, but we also knew that we could lose the entire Tour on this stage.

We started the stage in the rain, and 300 meters into the race, Chechu Rubiera's front wheel slid out directly in front of me. I thought we were going to crash, but we didn't. It was amazing that he stayed upright. We continued at a relatively conservative pace. But we ended up dropping one of our riders before the first time check. Normally, this would not be a big deal, but we have always finished with every rider in the TTT. That's been something that is important to the team. You don't have to finish all nine riders, as the time for the team is taken on the fifth rider at the finish. But we've always finished all our riders in the TTT, due to the strength of our team. Many teams drop riders in the TTT because their team is not as strong.

Dropping one of our riders was a little extra stress on an already very stressful stage. Our pace turned out to be too conservative when we were 40 seconds down at the first time split. This was only 19 kilometers into a 64.5-kilometer (40-mile) race. We had some work to do, and we knew it. Fortunately, none of us panicked, and we gradually increased our speed. We got into a rhythm, and by the second time check, we had erased our deficit. We were back on track to win the stage. We gradually increased our speed over the last half of the race, and we killed everyone. We beat the second-place team by more than a minute in a race that normally has a winning margin of seconds. Our team had worked together as a unit to achieve our goal. It was a great stage victory and an excellent example of superior teamwork.

Assembling the fastest individual riders in the world has never been the most important thing for the team. Our team has to gel. We want the best team we can have. That includes everyone and not just the riders. U.S. Postal has assembled the best team behind the scenes as well. Everyone in the team cars, everyone in the bus—coaches, management, chefs, mechanics, massage therapists, everyone—is dedicated to the team. Everyone has to play a role, and there has to be chemistry. You can't always win unless you have cohesion. Think about the U.S. men's basketball team in Athens: They were the best individual players in the world, but they just couldn't play together as a team to win the most important games. Several other teams, with greater team unity, were able to come together and beat the best individual players in the world. Good teamwork can be powerful.

Starting last of all the teams in the 2004 Tour, U.S. Postal had the advantage, since they had time split references for all the other teams who'd already raced. Each rider on our team wears a radio during the team time trial so they have information from Johan at all times throughout the event. The team started off slower than most of their major adversaries in the race, which was a good tactic as they didn't have to take any risks in the wet corners and could settle into a good rhythm. They then picked up their speed progressively to be fastest by the midpoint. The team dominated the stage, never showing weakness and bettering all of the other teams by over a minute. Lance in yellow, the team on the podium with a victory—it was an incredible race under horrible weather conditions.

Racing in the rain is never much fun, and racing a team time trial in the rain is particularly nerve-racking. Many teams suffered crashes and flat tires throughout the race and lost precious seconds to their competitors. It is always interesting to see if a team will wait for a rider when he crashes or gets a flat. The decision depends on which rider has had problems and where the team is at in the race. For example, if any of the riders puncture a tire early in the race, the team will usually wait because that rider will most likely be a benefit to the team later on. However, if the rider punctures near the end of the event, the team will just push on to the finish, unless, of course, it's the team's leading rider. If the team leader crashes or punctures, everybody on the team will wait for him to get back up and into the team line. If a weaker rider has problems, the team may just decide to keep on going no matter what point of the race it is.

For example, in the TTT, Benjamin couldn't hold the pace of the team and was left behind early on. He had crashed in each of the prior two stages and was banged up, and he would most likely have been sore in the TTT and not able to ride strongly. Therefore, once he was dropped from the team, they plowed on toward the finish and left him to reach the line on his own steam. It was sad to see him get dropped, because he would have been a great asset to the team under normal circumstances.

Several teams did experience multiple flat tires in the TTT, but our team didn't have one. The night before the event Johan and Dirk paid close attention to the weather forecast, and when it was near certain there would be rain, the mechanics changed the tires on the bikes from 19-millimeter tubulars to 20-millimeter tires—the larger tires are less likely to puncture and also handle much better in wet conditions. The larger surface area is slightly less aerodynamic, but this disadvantage is far outweighed by the advantages under these circumstances. Both the Phonak and CSC teams opted for the smaller tires. As a result, they had many punctured tires, and several riders slid out in the corners.

Because each team starts the TTT with nine riders but only the first five riders' times count for the team's time at the finish, this can create a special predicament. Phonak, Tyler Hamilton's team, had only five riders left going into the final kilometers of the race. If one of the remaining five riders would have had a mishap and lost time, the final rider's time would have been the time of the team. Thankfully, for them, nothing happened and their five riders crossed the finish line in a group.

The TTT victory was great for Postal because it was a team victory from start to finish. I know how hard all these guys worked since the start of the season, and it was thrilling to see them come across the line smiling with their fists punched toward the sky.

After the TTT, Lance was in yellow for the first time in the 2004 Tour. In the next stage, though, the team chose not to waste much

CASEY B. GIBSON

IN FORMATION: *Viatcheslav Ekimov leads his cycling partners in the team time trial.*

energy defending his lead and let a breakaway of five cruise up the road and gain many minutes on the peloton. Lance could afford to let a few riders who weren't contenders get away and take time on him in the overall classification in the early, flat stages, since they can eventually lose lots of time in the mountain stages. The team is better off saving energy for the mountains, where they tend to gain a lot of time. It is a good tactic that saves the team energy for the later weeks.

CHAPTER TEN

JERSEYS & REST DAYS WORTH RACING FOR

When the Tour de France was initially sponsored by the French newspaper *L'Auto*, the race leader's jersey was chosen to be yellow, the color of the newspaper's pages. Similarly, the Tour of Italy has a pink jersey for its leader. Pink was chosen for that race because the main sponsor, the sports newspaper *La Gazzetta dello Sport*, has pink pages.

In the Tour there are several leader's jerseys with different colors and designs that are handed out on the podium at the end of each stage. The yellow jersey is the Golden Fleece of the lot, the one that every racer wants to wear because it carries the most prestige. Yellow signifies which rider is leading the overall classification, based on the least amount of accumulated time for the stages raced. The white jersey is also based on the overall classification but is given to the best-placed rider under 25 years of age.

During the stages, races within the race always occur, where the riders sprint for prizes at different points in the stages. This competitive element was created to add excitement to the race and provide extra opportunities for the riders to chase. The towns that line the courses draw large numbers of spectators, so the "sprint" lines also add excitement for the fans. The green jersey is awarded to the rider who has accumulated the most points in the sprints during the race and has also placed the most consistently at the stage finishes. Within the Tour, there is a continual sprinter's competition for the green jersey at each stage.

Another competition within the race is for the polka-dot jersey, which is awarded to the rider who reaches the summit of the climbs in the front the most frequently. The climbs along the course are categorized based on difficulty, with more points being awarded for the bigger mountains in the Alps and Pyrénées and fewer points for the small *bergs* in Belgium. The rider who reaches Paris at the end of the race with the jersey still on his back is the overall winner. Frenchman Richard Virenque has won this competition more than any other rider in the peloton and set a record with seven victories in 2004.

Thomas Voeckler took over the yellow jersey in the first week of the 2004 Tour and held on to it for nearly half of the race. Voeckler was the French national champion, so he normally raced with a blue, white, and red jersey signifying that he is France's national champion. There are other national champions in the peloton who can be distinguished by the fact that they are not wearing their team's colors but their country's colors.

There is also a team classification based on the overall time of the top three riders of that team on each stage. These stage times are added together, and a prize is given to the most consistent team at the finish in Paris. Prior to cyclists wearing hard-shell helmets, the leading team would wear yellow caps. Now leading is no longer distinguished within the peloton during the race and is instead presented to the public prior to the start each morning.

Voeckler's team, Brioches la Boulangère, was ecstatic with his yellow jersey while racing through Brittany, close to the French team's home base. La Boulangère is a commercial bakery that makes all those tasty pastries the French are famous for. In the peloton there are hundreds of different sponsors, from Gerolsteiner water to Crédit Agricole banks, representing countries from all over the world. Their colorful logos are emblazoned on the various team jerseys

The French riders and the French teams were in particularly good form in the 2004 Tour. It is always important for the Tour and for cycling in France for the French riders to put on a good show in their home race. They did just that. They were always well represented at the front of the peloton in the stage finishes. The French Crédit Agricole team won a stage with a solid team effort in the final kilometers of the race. Thor Hushovd, its Norwegian sprinter, not only wore the yellow jersey but also won a stage, and the yellow jersey lay firmly on the shoulders of Voeckler for ten days.

Cycling is a sport that carries on in all conditions; there are no rain delays, time-outs, or yellow flags. During the first week of the Tour, we saw numerous crashes in which massive bunches of riders piled into one another unable to stop quickly enough on the wet roads. Their tires were sliding out from underneath them like shoes on an ice rink.

In the first week and a half of racing, it was very windy. A strong wind can be as detrimental as a mountain pass to a rider not prepared for it. Johan is constantly aware of the different directions the course is going to take while we are racing. He alerts us over the radio to any potentially volatile situations in which the wind can split the peloton. Racing in the wind is always tough, since it requires full and constant concentration. Gaps in the peloton are created quickly when it is windy, and riders can end up chasing for 100 kilometers (62 miles) or more if they are inattentive for just a few seconds.

Prior to the start of the race, the *soigneurs* drive ahead to the feed zone and stage finish. Once en route they'll call Johan and alert him to any dangers that lie ahead, such as wet and slippery sections, narrow roads, steep climbs, dangerous descents, or areas of strong wind.

Drafting is a key tactical element to bicycle racing. With a stiff wind it becomes even more crucial to be well positioned. The most dangerous situation for the peloton is when a crosswind is blowing. A direct tail wind or head wind tends to keep the peloton intact, but a crosswind can splinter the peloton, when weaker riders become unable to hold the wheel in front of them while fighting the wind from the side. In a crosswind, the peloton will form echelons across the road where the riders are diagonally staggered one behind the next to gain maximum protection from the wind. The situation becomes dangerous when a team goes to the front of the peloton, forms an echelon, and then doesn't allow any riders in the draft with them.

The first hours of the race, those that are not televised live due to the length of the stages, are often the craziest. Riders will attack from the start on the flat stages to create a breakaway. The team with the yellow jersey will attempt to control which breakaways gain time and which need to be brought back—they will not let riders who might threaten their hold on the yellow jersey gain any time on the bunch, but they will allow a breakaway of riders far down on the classification to gain a controlled amount of time. Once the break is established, the race usually settles down, the attacks stop, and the leading team rides a steady speed on the front to keep the race in its control. When they begin to close in on the finish, the sprinters' teams will take over on the front and attempt to bring the breakaway back so that their sprinter can have a shot at the stage victory.

After the first week of the 2004 Tour, I was sure some of the riders were beginning to count the days until they got to the mountains. The racing was incredibly stressful. In each stage a few more riders were forced to abandon the race due to injuries sustained in crashes. Once the riders hit the slopes of the Pyrénées, the race for the overall would begin to sort itself out; riders would tire out, with many no longer able to fight for position in the bunch, and the tension would abate somewhat. I think the people most nervous watching the Tour are all the mothers and wives following their sons and husbands during the racing, praying they make it through each day without a crash.

> *CHRISTIAN DESCRIBED THE FINISH LIKE A WRESTLING CAGE MATCH—THE BARRIERS THAT LINED THE ROAD ON EITHER SIDE LEFT NO ROOM FOR ESCAPE.*

I spoke with Christian at the end of the first week. He had crashed in a massive pileup the day before and said he never touched the ground when he crashed since there were already so many riders already lying there. Being from the home of the Chicago Bears NFL team he described his tumble as a "Walter Payton," saying the finish was like a wrestling cage match—the barriers that lined the road on either side left no room for escape. There was not one rider on his Liberty Seguros team who didn't crash in the first week of the race. Most had pretty bad battle scars to show for it. Most of the peloton was in the same boat as his team.

The race left the flatlands and headed south toward the Pyrénées, and as I watched the race on television, I could tell the peloton had lost a bit of its spark. Some of the riders were not pedaling quite as smoothly as they had been a few days ago. Riding in the rain and wind on small French roads will suck some of the gas out of the engine.

Racing in the rain is tough, even for guys who grow up training and racing in foul weather. It seems as if the riders faced either pounding rain or a slight drizzle for most of the first week of the Tour. Judging by the clothing the riders had layered over their jerseys, it was not a warm rain. Whenever riders have arm warmers, vests, or rain jackets on, you know it must be cold—especially when they don't shed them in the final kilometers of the race as things begin to heat up.

Racing in wet weather is tense also because dirty road water is constantly being thrown up into your face from the rider's wheel in front of you for hours on end. You can't see much and your eyes get sore. Sunglasses or goggles don't really work, because they get covered in grit and dirt from the road and fog up, so visibility is even more limited.

CSC rider Jakob Piil was the great animator of the flat stages of the Tour in 2004. His tenacity to keep pushing and making the breakaways each day in the start of the race was impressive. It is not easy to make the breakaway, as a good portion of the peloton is trying to get in one that stays up front. He never achieved a stage victory and ended up getting a bad case of tendinitis after the incredible workload he assumed in the first 10 days of the race, which was a shame because he deserved accolades for all his effort. I am certain his team was happy that their sponsors' logos were in front and on TV for hours at a time.

Jakob lives just outside of Girona on the Mediterranean coast. He came to Spain with several other Danish CSC teammates to escape the cold of northern Europe. Jakob is a good guy, shy and quiet. He is also an extremely talented bike racer. After transitioning from the track to the road, he has won a stage of the Tour and is famous in America for his victory in Philadelphia's USPRO Championship.

Some riders in the peloton count down the kilometers until each rest day, whereas others are just starting to find their rhythm. A day without racing makes them feel sluggish when they return to the race. A "rest day" isn't really a complete day of rest for the riders, since they will still be on their bikes for a couple of hours of light training. If they didn't ride a little, their legs would seize up and would be sore and painful at the start of the next stage. The ride on a rest day, even though it will be upward of two hours, doesn't tire out the racers but simply keeps their bodies moving at the familiar pace and keeps their legs loose. If you take the day off the bike, your body will think it is time to recover instead of time to keep going.

The UCI mandates that races three weeks in length have two rest days, due to the physical demands of bicycle racing for three weeks at a time. The rest days are forced, so that the riders don't push themselves beyond their physical limits. Whether the rest days make any physical difference at the end of a three-week race is questionable, but they do provide a mental break for the riders.

Some riders in the peloton ride for a couple of hours at an extremely leisurely pace on rest days, while others ride three hours or so at a steady speed with some intensity. I know Lance likes to ride at a hard tempo on rest days. Since the team rides together with team cars following behind, the few guys who don't want to ride quite as hard may hold on to or draft a team car to preserve their strength.

Generally, the team draws an entourage of reporters, television cameras, and team cars around them during the training ride. The rest day gives the media a chance to get shots of the team away from the race and also to get interviews with riders and summary quotes about the preceding week of racing.

As there is no structured schedule on rest days until training begins that day, everybody tends to sleep in a little later and hang around the breakfast table a little longer. The riders continue eating the same foods and quantities, since their metabolisms are high and they need the fuel to recover from the day before and to stock up for the next day.

Often a few friends join the U.S. Postal training ride during the rest day. In 2003 Robin Williams joined the team for the ride and raised everyone's spirits with his humor. The team is so incredibly strong that the invited riders don't hang on for long. At the 2002 Vuelta a España, Chechu Rubiera invited his friend Fernando Alonso to come along. Alonso wasn't yet the Formula 1 superstar he is today, and so the media crush he experiences today was not a factor. He was able to ride with the team for a few hours. He is a fit athlete, a cycling fan, and often trains on the bike to get ready for car races. When asked who his hero is he responded, "Miguel Induráin."

The biggest relief from having a day off is the fact that the riders don't have to pack their bags, pin their numbers, get in the bus and travel to the start, or deal with all the chaos in and around the race. The time away also provides a day of recovery for all the riders with injuries. On race days, it is hard to focus on healing injuries or getting them checked out because there is so much going on. On a day off, injured riders can ice their bumps a little longer, have a more thorough massage, stretch a little longer, and see the doctor or the chiropractor.

The first rest day in the 2004 Tour was truly enjoyed by the peloton, since in the first week of the race everyone had devoted a lot of energy to fighting for position in the bunch and trying to avoid crashes. By the second rest day, everyone was trying to recover after several days of intense physical effort in the Pyrénées. They wanted to build up as much energy as possible for the Alps looming in the next days.

The first week of racing was basically one of conservative racing for Lance and the team. They were saving their energy for an assault on the Pyrénées and Alps. The team came out of the first 10 days well. Lance was once again looking like the man most likely to conquer the mountains and take over the yellow leader's jersey.

CHAPTER ELEVEN

UP THE PYRÉNÉES

*D*uring the flat stages, it was crucial to keep Lance fresh and out of trouble, away from crashes. Since the team had done this perfectly, he arrived in the Pyrénées in great form and gained a significant time advantage on most of his competitors. Lance and the team had been prepared for the worst in northern Europe, and due to the energy they saved from being prepared for any circumstance, they were at ease in the mountains. It was crucial that Lance hit the Pyrénées with a bang to cause a blow to the morale of his opponents before they hit the Alps.

Riding in the peloton, it is fairly easy to recognize which riders are truly fit and which riders are struggling with the pace. Riders who are fit and fresh can accelerate quickly and pedal smoothly. Their bodies remain motionless while their legs turn over the pedals comfortably, and they are breathing without laboring. During the 2002 and 2003 seasons I rode the Vuelta with Roberto Heras. Roberto is a snappy climber. When he is in form he jumps around the peloton like a

Mexican jumping bean. It was hard to keep track of him in the bunch, but every so often we'd see him jump out of the draft and into the wind and accelerate up the side of the peloton. His change in style on the bike is tremendous between when he is bopping around in the Vuelta and when he is struggling at the training camps in the early season.

As the race moves into the mountains, the fans see a whole new set of riders attempting to win stages. The sprinters of the first week are simply trying to make it to the finish so that they can start the following stage, whereas the skinny little climbers who have been hiding within the bunch on the flat stages are now flying up the hills, comfortable in their element. The race for the sprinter's green jersey cools while the battle for the polka-dot climber's jersey heats up.

The first day of long climbs in the high mountains always offers a few surprises. Prior to the Pyrénéan test, the mountains were not high enough for the climbers in the peloton to get a true read on one another. But once the peloton hit steep ascents, the race exploded. At that point, Lance all but eliminated most of his rivals, although he also found a few unexpected ones.

It is a shock to all the riders' systems when they begin climbing the first big mountains of the race. The first day of climbing feels like jumping into water after a long time without swimming—it's a bit scary, you flounder and splash and have horrible form, but after a few moments it all comes back and the body recalls what it knows how to do. For certain, many riders finished the first stage in the mountains on their hands and knees. As predicted, the peloton did break apart on the climbs, leaving the sprinters and *rouleurs* (a French word given to a rider who is comfortable rolling along at high speed in a big gear on flatter terrain) behind while the climbers rode in their element up front.

The first ray of intense sunshine hit the Tour at about the halfway mark. Instead of constantly going back to the team cars for their rain jackets to keep the water off, the riders were going back for water bottles to keep themselves hydrated and cool. During a race in the heat, the riders constantly drink, consuming on average a bottle of either water or energy drink every half hour. The changes in temperature also cause many riders to catch colds and get sick—it can be a roller coaster for the immune system.

While racing in the heat, it is hard to consume food but easy to drink fluids, whereas in the cold and wet weather it is easier to eat but harder to drink. Oftentimes I need to remind myself to drink in the cold, and in the heat I simply consume Clif Shots, since they are easy to get down and digest on a hot day. The *soigneurs* will put gels in the freezer for the riders before a race in the heat. I'll tell you, a cold chocolate gel tastes really good during a hot race in the sun.

A nice feature in the Tour that we don't get to enjoy in other events is the bottle motorbike. Among the Tour's sponsors is Aquarel mineral water, which has motorcycles in the race that buzz around with baskets of water on the back. The riders in the breakaway can pull drinks off of the bikes to refresh themselves in case their team cars are not around to give them service. More than once I have found myself in a breakaway without a drink, my mouth stuck dry and my skin getting goose bumps and an occasional shiver. At times like these, water is all you crave and the race seems secondary.

In the last 20 kilometers of each stage, the team cars are not allowed to provide food or drink to the riders. I think this rule makes sure the cars are not able to help the riders in any way by drafting them or towing them in the final part of the race. It would also be dangerous to have riders going back for bottles or cars coming up, as the racers gallop to the finish. Occasionally a rider will take a feed from the car in dire situations, and doing so causes the team director to be fined by the *commissaires*; usually it is a fine of 50 Swiss francs, which makes for an expensive bottle of water or can of Coke.

The last rider in the overall classification is called the *lanterne rouge,* which comes from the red lantern that hung on the back of the caboose at the end of a train. It has become a bit of an honor to win the *lanterne*, and often there is even a competition among the last riders in the peloton.

On smaller winding roads, riding in the front of the peloton is significantly easier because there is an elastic effect when the group comes out of a corner or over a small hill. The slowing of speed and acceleration is exponential the farther back a rider is, which means the last riders are almost always doing more work to stay in the group than the riders at the front. On the smaller climbs, sprinters who are trying to survive in the peloton for as long as possible also will start the climb at the front, giving themselves some space to drift through the peloton on the way up the climb, whereas if they were at the back, they'd be dropped straightaway.

> *IT HAS BECOME A BIT OF AN HONOR TO WIN THE LANTERNE ROUGE, AND OFTEN THERE IS EVEN A COMPETITION AMONG THE LAST RIDERS IN THE PELOTON.*

In the mountain stages, Lance and the team opted for lighter bikes and wheels because they didn't want to carry any extra weight uphill. The technology the U.S. Postal team has at its disposal is the best in the peloton—the bikes are light but stiff, the wheels fast and light yet strong, and the helmets cool yet protective. These features are extremely important when you're on the bike six hours a day and racing up to the summits of mountain peaks. The Trek frames and Bontrager wheels are both made of carbon fiber and the Giro helmets are carbon reinforced. Carbon fiber is light, stiff, and sturdy, and has become the material of choice in bicycle technology, as well as many other sports. The Trek Madone bike the team rides was designed using our sponsor's AMD computer processors, providing technology that gives the Postal team an advantage.

Triki, Floyd, Chechu, and José were all riding gray and white bikes in the mountain stages. These bikes are similar to the blue and white ones that George and the others were riding, but they are even lighter. They have no paint and are natural carbon in the back, which lightens them up by 100 or so grams. The UCI has a rule that the bikes cannot be under a certain weight, 6.8 kilograms (14.99 pounds), so the bikes the team was using for the mountains were right at the limit of weight; any lighter and the bikes would be considered illegal for competition.

Although it is now mandatory to wear a helmet in the professional peloton, if the race finishes on the top of a mountain, the riders can discard their helmets at the base of the final climb. On a mountain, the speeds are slow and your body heats up quickly. It was determined by the UCI that the cool comfort of a bare head outweighs the safety the helmet might provide on a mountain ascent. When the race finishes at the top of a mountain, Johan tells the riders over the radio where they can drop their helmets and team staff are positioned on the side of the road, ready to receive them. At the bottom of the climbs, the riders can be seen dumping their helmets. It is a bit dodgy for the staff picking

THE ACE: *José Azevedo charges up a climb at the '04 Tour de France.*

up the helmets, especially when the team is hammering away on the front, as they have five or six helmets coming at them from all angles.

Getting ready for my first race as a five-year-old, I strapped on a slightly large leather helmet—the protective material was leather stuffed with padding and sewn together to form sausage-like bands running lengthwise across the rider's head. In North America, the helmets were called "hairnets," because they looked sort of like hairnets and only provided a fraction more protection. In France, the helmets were called *casque à boudin*, or sausage helmets. Until the summer of 2003, when the new rules came into effect, the soft helmets were still in use in the peloton by some die-hard, old-school professionals. The days of the "hairnet," cotton hat, or flying hair in the wind are over. Helmets have evolved immensely over time. The rules on helmet usage began to change in the amateur peloton in the 1980s, making it almost inevitable that the pros would follow suit, which they soon did.

U.S. Postal looked great through the Pyrénées. The team kept the race in control and set the stages up perfectly for Lance. The goal was to gain time on as many of Lance's rivals in the overall as possible without riders taxing themselves too much since they would face an even tougher course in the Alps the next week. Lance made some attacks but they were not as ferocious as the attacks we have seen in past Tours as he could rely on his performance in the time trials to gain time on his rivals.

Lance managed to gain a lot of time on two of his main rivals, Jan Ullrich and Tyler Hamilton. Neither could handle the pace set by Chechu and José. Hamilton abandoned, and Ullrich was dropped quite close to the bottom of the final ascent. More than a loss of time, this was a blow to their confidence in the mountain stages ahead.

Lance had said that the stage to the Pyrénéan mountaintop, Plateau de Beille, was one incredibly hard stage—"inhumane" he called it—but he also said that he loved it.

As the mountain stages passed each day, the team continued to put in an incredible performance from start to finish, proving it not only had the strongest rider in the race but also the strongest team to lead and protect Lance through the entire three weeks. Each day the team rode on the front, setting a tempo that slowly whittled away the peloton. Riders were dropped over every climb: first the sprinters came off the back of the group, then the strong flatlanders, then some climbers, then Lance's big rivals, until there was only Ivan Basso and a few pink T-Mobile jerseys left in the team's wake.

In the team meetings prior to the mountain stages, Johan decides which guys on the team will be used on the front when and where during a race. Ekimov and Pavel Padrnos are both workhorses who can cruise at a fast and steady pace on the flats, so they were used in the valleys between the mountain passes to keep the tempo high and the race in their control. Triki and Noval are both comfortable on the climbs, so their energy was applied to set a tempo on the first climbs of the day. George, Floyd, Chechu, José, and Lance all rode in their wake on the front, saving their energy for the final assaults on the competitors and the climbs later in the race. During the mountain stages José was usually the last rider on the team to pull; when he finished his work Lance was left with one rider to deal with in the last kilometers of the race.

When the team rides a steady and hard speed on the front, they eliminate riders due to the speed but they also keep the riders who are a threat under control. When the speed is high, it is useless for any of their rivals to attack, because they will not be able to gain much ground on the lead team. Then the team will simply cooperate, sharing the work in the wind to bring the breakaway back. Only when the team that is leading shows signs of weakness will other riders try to attack. Very few tried to attack the team through the Pyrénées. Those who did didn't get too far up the road and wasted energy.

It is said in the peloton that a race leader's jersey and, in particular, the yellow jersey gives a rider wings. As groups of riders came off the back of the peloton during each mountain stage, the yellow jersey–clad Voeckler looked as if he would get dropped with each pitch in gradient, but he kept fighting all the way to the line. The yellow jersey had given him the wings he needed to climb better than he ever had before. The French found a new cycling hero, and they carried him up the climbs with their encouragement. It was awesome to see a young rider fight through the pain in his legs and keep pushing to the bitter end. When so many other riders lose motivation due to the intense pain of lactic acid built up in their legs and from damage to their muscles, Voeckler pushed on, grimacing all the way to the finish line. His fierce accelerations to get back onto the leading groups were amazing. I know the pain he must have felt. To block it out and push over the top of it was incredible. He fought for the yellow jersey with everything he had and rode like a champion of the sport. The jersey looked much brighter on his back each day as a result.

IT IS SAID IN THE PELOTON THAT A RACE LEADER'S JERSEY AND, IN PARTICULAR, THE YELLOW JERSEY GIVES A RIDER WINGS.... THE YELLOW JERSEY–CLAD VOECKLER LOOKED AS IF HE WOULD GET DROPPED WITH EACH PITCH IN GRADIENT, BUT HE KEPT FIGHTING ALL THE WAY TO THE LINE.

During **the** **T**our often a Hollywood star or famous musician will take a stroll through the bus to shake hands with the riders for support. In 2003, Arnold Schwarzenegger followed the Tour for a few days to promote *Terminator 3*, one of his movies being released in Europe soon after the Tour. He couldn't make it down the aisle in the bus because he was too wide and had to turn sideways to get to the back and shake all the riders' hands. Since Lance brought cycling into the international limelight over the past six years, stars are using the Tour and Lance as a vehicle to promote their movies. At the finish line in

Paris in 2004, actor Will Smith was on the Champs-Elysées to shake the riders' hands as they stepped down from the podium. Also on the bus during the Tour was musician Ben Harper, who was touring through the area and thought it would be cool to check out the race.

The team came out of the Pyrénées in a better position than anyone would have imagined. Lance had narrowed the list of riders that could threaten him in the race overall and the team was very strong, healthy, and generally doing better than any other team in the race.

CHAPTER TWELVE

INTO THE ALPS

*A*fter two long, hard days in the mountains, the riders had a shorter flat day along the southern edge of France. The race had gone over three-quarters of the lap, or Tour, of France and was on its way back up to Paris. But the Alps still needed to be climbed.

I kept in contact with the U.S. Postal staff and the riders throughout the Tour. The team had ridden incredibly well in the first two weeks of the race and had accomplished what they set out to do in the first part of the race. But they were all quick to point out that the final week was going to be exceptionally difficult, and a lot could still go wrong. Lance could have a bad day or a mishap and another rider could have a fantastic day. Things could change quickly in the overall standings. Lance and the team never say the race is won until the line is crossed in Paris. In cycling, you can never count on a win until the race is finished.

Between the mountain stages, the riders had just one flat day of racing on their way up to the Alps. Bike racers have an attack-until-death mentality. Even though there was not one fresh rider in the peloton who was eager to attack from the gun, they all knew that in the flat stages there was a good chance that a breakaway could make it to the finish. So a good percentage of the peloton wanted to get into a breakaway that would stay away and have a chance at a stage victory. Eventually a break does get away, and then the peloton is more than happy to settle into its own speed, while the breakaway races for the stage victory up the road.

The directors driving in the race caravan following the peloton have to be attentive at all times and need to be skilled drivers. When cyclists are getting dropped or are coming back for bottles, they are between the cars, and it gets chaotic. Often, when there is a good moment in the race and it's not too fast or undulating, there will be an exodus of riders to the back of the peloton to get bottles for their teammates. When a rider gets to the back of the group, he'll raise his hand in the air and call for his team car that he needs water, Coke, or food. The *commissaires* will signal over the race radio what team cars can come forward. The order is based on which riders get their hands up first. Inevitably, there is a jam of riders and cars at the back of the peloton, all dodging each other while trying to give or receive service. Riders negotiate through a tangle of cars with five or six bottles in the backs of their jerseys, maybe two in the front and sometimes one in hand—it's quite acrobatic and a little touch-and-go at times.

There is a mechanic in the backseat of the team car, ready with his toolbox and a set of spare wheels at his side in case a rider has mechanical problems or needs a bike or wheel change. Beside the director there may be a guest of the team or just one of the team staff along for the ride—the front passenger seat is usually just that, a passenger seat. Johan will be listening to the race radio that is broadcast from the race directors' cars, which gives the specifics of the race and directions to all the team cars. They announce the time gaps of break-aways, the riders' numbers in the breakaways, and dangers coming up on the course. Johan relays this information to the riders over a separate set of radios tuned to their own channel. Ahead on the course, the *soigneurs* will be both at the finish and in the feed zone and call Johan about any tight corners or unexpected dangers, climbs, or other hazards on the course. There is also a television in the team car tuned into the race so that the directors always know what is going on in the front of the peloton and how all the riders are looking.

After two weeks of racing, most of the riders are ready to be done with the race and get home with their families. Two weeks is enough, and the end usually still seems quite a distance away. The riders spend three days together prior to the race and then three weeks together during the race. All the guys are great friends, and the staff are fantastic as well, but three weeks of being with the same people 24 hours a day tends to become too much.

In three-week races, consistency is crucial. An incredible day on the bike can quickly be eclipsed by a horrible day. Lance had been unbelievably consistent through the first two weeks of the Tour. He had been careful to use his teammates wisely, saving their energy as much as his. He knows from experience that he needs each team member to be strong in the last week as well.

Before the Tour, Lance said the team would need to be especially strong in the last week because it would be so grueling. It is usual to see some riders do incredibly well in the last week and to see some of the stars of the first two weeks falter. The racing had been tough—the extremes in weather during the previous two weeks combined with crashes and tough mountain days had depleted a lot of riders for the final week.

The race exploded as they climbed back up into the mountains. Attacks fractured the peloton, but Lance was back in yellow after the first day in the high Alps. He had a firm grasp on the lead, and he had no intention of letting up before reaching the finish line in Paris.

To scout out l'Alpe d'Huez, Lance, his archrival Ivan Basso, and the other riders headlining the race had ridden up the legendary ascent several times before the Tour. For this time trial stage, it is crucial for riders to know every inch of the road, how the 21 switchbacks on the climb need to be approached, and how they should gauge their efforts during the race. Before the racers even got to this stage, Lance had memorized the climb and would be able to visualize the entire climb in his head and how he would ascend it.

Not only have the riders been preparing for the climb by riding up and down it repeatedly, but their bikes and equipment have been created for this event as well. Teams of engineers and designers worked on Lance's uphill time trial bike for months to give him the greatest technical advantage possible for his assault on the climb. The bikes were all right on the 6.8-kilogram weight allowance imposed by cycling's governing body. Lance rode on superlight carbon fiber wheels that are also extremely aerodynamic. While using these wheels, a rider can accelerate much faster out of the corners, which is a great advantage on this climb. Nike has developed incredibly light shoes for the uphill time trial; rotational weight of the feet is even more crucial on a climb, since the rider lifts his feet with every pedal stroke.

Both Roberto Heras's and Lance's bikes actually ended up weighing in slightly under the legal limit for this stage, so their respective team mechanics had to add some extra ounces before they were launched from the start house. They simply had to put on an extra water bottle cage and another roll of handlebar tape. The mechanics had weighed Lance's bike at the team truck prior to the official weigh-in, and the bike had been spot on, but the official scale was not being recalibrated with each bike check, and so they may have been getting skewed readings.

THROUGHOUT THE TOUR, LANCE AND THE TEAM RECEIVED SEVERAL THREATS FROM ANONYMOUS CALLERS.

Throughout the Tour, Lance and the team received several threats from anonymous callers. They could have easily been idle threats from drunken fans wanting to scare the team out of racing, but they could not be taken lightly. L'Alpe d'Huez is the riskiest of stages, and Lance would be alone riding up a climb with swarms of people inches away from him. There was no way the police could search every car or barricade on the entire climb. For every 100 fans cheering, there may be one nasty spectator booing, spitting on, or threatening Lance and the team. Unfortunately that person sometimes gets the attention he's seeking.

Mountain time trials are entirely different from a flat time trial, in that the rider must have a high power-to-weight ratio, a huge lung capacity, and a high pain threshold. On the climbs during the mountain stages, riders in the front group are riding at approximately 6 or more watts per kilogram of weight. A rider of 70 kilograms produces about 420, or more, watts on l'Alpe d'Huez. It is remarkable that riders can compete at those wattages over five or six hours in a stage after having already raced for two weeks.

Mountain time trials are ruthless; if a rider has an off day he can lose many minutes. The sprinters race as hard as possible as well—not to win the stage but to simply make the time cut of 33 percent. If a rider's time is 33 percent slower than the winner's, they cannot start the following stage and are out of the race. The modern-era riders who are in the first places have the lightest equipment available to them and not a scrap of fat on their bodies. The uphill effort is the purest of physical tests, with the best athlete usually winning.

Because the time trial is uphill and similar to a mountaintop finish of a road stage, helmets are not mandatory. As a result, most of the riders opted to ride up the mountain with their hair in the wind. An aerodynamic time trial helmet would be too hot to wear for the event, since those helmets don't have much ventilation and also tend to be heavy.

While in training, Lance tests himself often in the mountains, as do most of the guys on the team. He takes on efforts similar to the Alpe d'Huez time trial to gauge his fitness. These training efforts are a great exercise because they can teach the rider how to maintain a consistent wattage, speed, and rhythm. Close to Girona there is an 8-kilometer climb that nearly all of the guys use for their intervals or fitness tests. The climb has a constant gradient of about 7 or 8 percent. On a weekday afternoon, there may be six of us going up and down that climb doing intervals. Prior to the Olympics, I joked that the town where the climb is located was Dede's second home as she was spending at least two hours a day riding up and down the slope.

Lance rides at a very high cadence when he is climbing. His style is somewhat unusual in the peloton as few riders can ride at such a high cadence and accelerate as fast out of the corners. Prior to joining U.S. Postal I would train with fairly big gears on my bike. I was convinced a 21 sprocket on the back was all I needed to climb a hill. After training with Lance a few times at camp and in Girona he told me I needed to change my rear cog. He noticed I only had a 21 on the back. He quickly suggested I fix a 25 on the back so that I could practice pedaling at a higher cadence. Days later, I had not yet put on a 25. He noticed and asked why I hadn't. I put one on my back hub that evening, and sure enough, the next day while training he noticed and was pleased that I had done so. After having trained with him a few times, I quickly realized why he liked the 25. Not only did he like to ride at a higher cadence, but he also likes to ride in the mountains often, even on days when he is taking it easy. Now I have a 25 on all of my training wheels, all of my teammates train with 25s, and I can spin my way up most mountains without straining my leg muscles too much.

In a mountainous time trial, it is crucial not to start too fast. A rider who builds up too much lactic acid in his legs in the early sections of the climb will be depleted in the latter part of the effort and simply come to pieces and lose a lot of time to other riders. The best tactic is to start out at a steady speed, find a fast rhythm, and then build to an all-out effort by the final kilometers of the race.

As an amateur, I trained and raced on many of the roads the Tour covered in the final Alps stages. It is an awesome area in which to ride

IN 2003, FLOYD HAD BAT-
TLED BACK FROM A BROKEN
FEMUR. IT WAS A BAD BREAK
AND ONE THAT COULD END A
CAREER, BUT HE MANAGED
TO RACE IN THE TOUR IN
2003 AND THEN COME BACK
AGAIN IN 2004 STRONGER
AND CLIMBING EVEN BETTER.

a bike, one of the best in the world, but at the same time, it is also one of the most challenging areas, due to the terrain. The climbs in the Alps are extremely demanding, so it was impressive to see the team arrive at the bottom of the last climb of the day still complete with nine riders, with only 50 riders able to follow their tempo. To have those numbers toward the end of a hard bike race is rare, and it put Lance in a comfortable position going into the final days of racing. With his team around him, he could rely on them to bring back any attack from a rival and to keep him protected from the wind.

In 2004, Floyd Landis showed his true capacities as a cyclist when the race was in the Alps. In 2003, he had battled back from a broken femur. It was a bad break and one that could end a career, but he managed to race in the Tour in 2003 and then come back again in 2004 stronger and climbing even better. After strong rides in the Alps and throughout the 2004 season in general, he was recruited by many teams and decided to leave our team for new experiences and opportunities with Phonak in 2005.

For the last six years, Postal's "blue train" has been on the front of the Tour de France peloton with the yellow jersey comfortably sitting last wagon. When Lance has the jersey, and even when he doesn't, the Postal boys ride to keep Lance in the front and out of trouble.

(ABOVE) *Michael Barry and Max Van Heeswijk lead the U.S. Postal squad to a brilliant victory in the opening team time trial stage of the 2004 Vuelta a España.*

(ABOVE) Manuel Beltran cranks out an espresso in preparation for another day of racing.

GRAHAM WATSON PHOTO

(RIGHT) Postal's team bus rolls into town with an entourage of excitement, not to mention riders, directors, equipment, and behind-the-scenes staff.

GRAHAM WATSON PHOTO

(ABOVE) *The low, winter light casts a stack of shadows as part of the Postal team embarks on an early-season ride at training camp in Solvang, California.*

ROBERT LABERGE/GETTY IMAGES

(LEFT) *Faithful domestique Chechu Rubiera shares a photo moment with boss Lance Armstrong during a quieter part of the 2004 Tour de France.*

GRAHAM WATSON PHOTO

(RIGHT) Colombian climber Daniel Rincon is known among his colleagues in the peloton for his willingness to ride hard in all conditions.

(BELOW) Seasoned Russian veteran Viatcheslav Ekimov, among cycling's most resilient and respected riders, has completed fourteen Tours de France, two short of the all-time record.

(ABOVE) Robbie Ventura, Damon Kluck, Floyd Landis, and Antonio Cruz relax prior to the 2004 USPRO Criterium Championship in Downer's Grove, near Chicago.

(LEFT) George Hincapie is the most consistent and strongest Postal rider in challenging cobblestone classics like Paris-Roubaix.

(RIGHT) Pavel Padrnos leads the Blue Train at the 2004 Dodge Tour de Georgia, which was won by Lance.

(ABOVE) Surrounded by Tour fanatics, José Azevedo powers to 4th place in the 2004 Tour's Alpe d'Huez time trial, 1:45 down on stage winner Lance Armstrong.

(ABOVE) Pavel Padrnos, George Hincapie, and Floyd Landis warm up prior to their winning effort in the team time trial at the 2004 Tour.

SAMMARYE LEWIS PHOTO

(LEFT) The race waits for no one: a Postal mechanic works on Joachim's derailleur during the 2004 Vuelta.

JAVIER SORIANO/AFP/GETTY IMAGES

(RIGHT, TOP) Johan Bruyneel has been Lance Armstrong's chief strategist (and alter ego) over six consecutive Tour de France wins.

GRAHAM WATSON PHOTO

(RIGHT, BOTTOM) Canadian mechanic Geoff Brown has been with the Postal team almost from the start.

SAMMARYE LEWIS PHOTO

(ABOVE) Colombian Victor Hugo Peña is a three-time veteran of Lance's Tour de France team. Although he rarely has opportunities for personal glory, Postal's victory in the 2003 team time trial put him in the yellow jersey for three days. He had more freedom at the 2003 Tour of Murcia, where he attacked (in the photo above), to win the stage.

(RIGHT) "I had great legs today, but I went to war . . . and lost," said Max Van Heeswijk after crashing within 30 kilometers of the finish of the 2003 Paris-Roubaix. "My front tire went flat, I had to step out of my pedal . . . and another rider ran into me." He still managed to finish the Hell of the North classic in 23rd place.

(CLOCKWISE FROM TOP) *Before taking up cycling, Victor Hugo Peña was called the Tiburon, or "the shark," for his talent as a swimmer.*

GRAHAM WATSON PHOTO

Floyd Landis is the king of wheelies—but he doesn't always keep his balance.

GRAHAM WATSON PHOTO

Wearing the Luxembourg national champion's jersey, Benoît Joachim shows all his power during the Tour of Flanders, one of the cobbled spring classics.

GRAHAM WATSON PHOTO

A staunch supporter of Lance and the team, actor Robin Williams is a regular at the Tour.

GRAHAM WATSON PHOTO

(LEFT) *A smile of relief from the author at the end of the 2004 Vuelta a España.*

GRAHAM WATSON PHOTO

(BELOW) *Michael Barry at an early race, before he ever shaved his legs.*

COURTESY OF THE AUTHOR

(BOTTOM) *Michael and his wife Dede join Canadian Gord Fraser and Team USA's Kristin Armstrong in the Athens Olympic Village cafeteria.*

COURTESY OF THE AUTHOR

(RIGHT) Chechu Rubiera celebrates Lance's sixth victory as he rides into Paris.

GRAHAM WATSON PHOTO

(BELOW) Assistant team director Dirk Demol boards the bus with Tour loot in hand.

SAMMARYE LEWIS PHOTO

(BOTTOM) U.S. fans watch on the frontline as the Postal team controls the pace in the '04 Tour.

JOEL SAGET/AFP/GETTY IMAGES

(RIGHT) Lance Armstrong takes time out at the back of the '04 Tour podium for a victory kiss from Sheryl Crow.

GRAHAM WATSON PHOTO

(BELOW) Chief mechanic Julien DeVriese hoses down a Discovery team bike in preparation for the 2005 season.

SAMMARYE LEWIS PHOTO

By the time the race reached the Alps, the peloton had thinned drastically. Riders had crashed, been injured, or simply had become depleted to their limits. The faces in the peloton were thin and the bodies skeletal, as the riders burned up far more calories than they were able to consume. Simply driving the route they had ridden would be tiring and depleting for most people.

At the end of a long stage race, it is hard to get your heart rate up and also difficult to pedal at a high cadence. It is more comfortable to turn over a bigger gear, since the legs are not as snappy due to all the muscle damage and stress of the repeated days of intense racing. It is harder to get the heart rate elevated as the body becomes increasingly tired.

Stage 19 of the 2004 Tour, at Besançon, was the final test for Lance in what is called the race of truth: the individual time trial. It has been said by the experts of the sport that to be a true champion of the Tour, to wear the yellow with honor, the leader must win the individual time trial. In 2004 Lance not only won the individual time trial but also the individual mountain time trial, and, fittingly, the team won the team time trial.

Johan is the only director in the peloton to have never lost a Tour de France. Johan came on board with U.S. Postal to help lead Lance and the team to their first Tour victory in 1999. Back then, both Lance and Johan were accomplished cyclists, but were rookies in Tour leadership. In five years they have learned from their mistakes and accomplishments and have formed the best Tour de France team in cycling around one of cycling's greatest champions.

The preceding year, in 2003, Lance came close to losing the Tour. At the end of the Tour, he said he would come back again in 2004 stronger and more prepared to battle the competition. He had his ups and downs leading up to the Tour in 2003 and was able to come back. Having learned from his mistakes, he was more confident, more prepared, and more relaxed to tackle the course and the competition.

As Lance left the start house for the final time trial in Besançon he looked calm and relaxed; his adversaries looked nervous and tense. His confidence could be seen in the way he approached the course, in the way he pounded the pedals. All he had to do was ride his hardest; he wasn't going to lose the yellow jersey, and there was a good chance he could win the stage. He was in a win-win position.

Floyd had a fantastic ride as well. He ripped through all the time checks to set the fastest times at that point, and gave Johan ideal reference points to relay to Lance. José, George, and Chechu, continuing the good performances the team had shown from the start of the race, all placed in the first 15.

Lance crushed his competitors in the time trial. His victory proved that he was the strongest in the Tour. Not only did he win on Alpe d'Huez, he would go on to dominate the flatter time trial a few days later. Lance and the team must have been able to sleep well knowing they had accomplished what no other cyclist ever has and knowing they faced no more battles in the Tour. As each rider finished the grueling stage and rolled across the line, it must have been a tremendous feeling. The team bus was now a party bus.

CHAPTER THIRTEEN

LES CHAMPS-ELYSÉES

*T*he finish line was crossed by the peloton on the Champs-Elysées in downtown Paris on July 25. Lance officially locked up his sixth Tour de France victory. The final lap of the Champs-Elysées is one the most satisfying hours in a cyclist's life. Simply finishing the Tour is a huge accomplishment, winning is incredible, and winning six in a row is legendary.

Tom Boonen of Belgium had the honor of winning the final stage of the Tour in front of hundreds of thousands of spectators lining this famous boulevard. Tom started out his career with U.S. Postal in 2002. He was coached and taught to race by Dirk Demol, U.S. Postal's second director, but was lured to the Quick Step team after having a stellar season with U.S. Postal. Tom has become a world-class sprinter and an ace in the early-season classic one-day races in Belgium and France.

When Tom arrived at U.S. Postal, we were all aware of his talents as a cyclist and his potential to be a champion. At our first training camp in Solvang, he lifted more weight on the leg press during a

CASEY B. GIBSON

HOME STRETCH: *Lance rides in the Tour's final stage, the Champs-Elysées.*

strength test than anybody else on the team, eventually reaching the machine's weight limit before he tired.

At our second camp, we were climbing hills each day and tuning our fitness. While climbing a 5-kilometer climb, Tom looked over at Christian and said, "This year I am not going to ride over the hills but through them." He was confident, not arrogant, and rode his way to several top places during the season, including an incredible third in Paris-Roubaix.

The Tour de France has not always finished on the Champs-Elysées. It used to finish in the velodrome of the Parc des Princes in Paris. The Tour now showcases the race and the riders by doing laps of the Champs-Elysées; the race up and down the avenue is essentially a lap of honor, in which the French public can see the champions of the Tour in its capital.

The Champs-Elysées is cobbled and slightly uphill, so it is not an easy road to race up and down. When riders attack, they race toward

CASEY B. GIBSON

PARADE LAP: *Beltran, Hincapie, and Landis celebrate a job well done.*

the paved gutters that line the side of the road, because they are much smoother than the cobbles and much faster. The peloton behind is too large for all riders to be in the gutters, so many riders are forced to bounce along on the cobbles, giving the riders in the breakaways a slight advantage. A challenge to riding the gutters is making sure your pedal doesn't hit the curb as it comes down on the stroke; in past years, this problem has caused a few riders to crash.

At the conclusion of the Tour ceremony, the team enjoyed a great party with everyone who has supported Lance and the team in pursuit of his Tour victories. The riders finally were reunited with their wives and loved ones after being separated for over three weeks.

Lance is the strongest athlete in the peloton. He is also the most driven and the most tactically astute. Johan and Lance never miss a detail. As a result, Lance achieved the greatest sporting feat in cycling history.

Lance in Girona: A Look Back

BY DEDE DEMET BARRY

When Michael started racing with U.S. Postal in 2002, we needed a European base and Girona was the logical choice to settle—several of his teammates and friends were there and travel to the races throughout Europe would be easily accessible with the Barcelona airport only an hour away.

Michael moved into an apartment with Dylan Casey and Christian Vande Velde. I came for the summer, after school was finished. I was racing that summer after a two-year break, and there was a tight cycling community in Girona—everyone would meet at the bridge in the center of town in the mornings for group rides.

One morning in August, I rolled down to the bridge with Dylan to meet the group for a ride, and Lance showed up. It was one week after his fourth Tour de France victory, and I had not seen him in a few years. Lance and I had first met at the world junior championships in 1989. We were both new to cycling; Lance had come from doing triathlons and I had been a speed skater. When I met him again in Girona that morning and we started pedaling and chatting, my thoughts floated back to Moscow and how our lives had changed since 1989.

The journey to Moscow had been long; I was one of the first American cyclists to arrive with the other track competitors, as I would race the pursuit before the road race. There was much talk about the hopes pinned on the men's team time trial, with Lance and 2004 Olympic medalist Bobby Julich leading the team. They arrived at our hotel a few days later, and I met Lance and his good friend and triathlon training partner, Chann McRae, for the first time as they were heading out for a 10-kilometer run, "to get the legs going and keep the tri form." Running tends to tighten up cyclist's legs, so we were all a bit surprised to see them heading out for a run a few days before the races, when every other cyclist in the competition would have been laying down with their legs in the air resting or spinning easy on their bike.

In the team time trial, Lance, as predicted, was far and away the strongest rider, and although they did not medal, they came close and put up a good fight. Lance went on to attack and break away in the first kilometer of the road race, ride off in the front the entire race with only one Russian kid to help, and then get caught on the final lap. Lance was by far the strongest in the race, and with a little tactical savvy, he would have won the race. Lance's performance in Moscow was one of the first signs that he was the most talented emerging cyclist in the world.

Lance was a brash kid from Texas who was aggressive and never afraid to be the boss among any group of people. He had fire in his eyes and loved to race. After his first year in the sport, he earned the nickname "King"; this is what he was called by both those who revered his talent and drive, as well as those who loathed his brash behavior.

Lance was self-focused, in a way that many great athletes and business people must be to become the best. Not everyone appreciated this, but he quickly garnered the respect of the cycling world as he fought his way to the front of every race. He blew nearly every race apart with his attacking style and had a burning desire to win at all costs.

From 1989 to 1993, when I spent time with Lance during national team events, he seemed two-dimensional; he was both an obsessive competitor, but also a laid-back kid from Texas who always enjoyed a Shiner Bock and good tunes.

After Lance won the world professional championships in 1993, we rarely crossed paths, as our cycling careers took us in different directions, although I always knew what he was up to. He was constantly making the news, winning a world championship, a million-dollar Triple Crown, competing in the Olympic Games, being stricken with cancer, and making an inspirational comeback from near death to win several Tours de France.

As we were pedaling along that August day through the Pyrénéan foothills, we laughed over how much our lives had changed since 1989. Lance had become a worldwide household name, and he was the proud father of three children. His interests were much more varied than the last time we had spoken. During the ride, he brushed me up on the history of Girona and Cataluña, and we spoke about the culture there, his keen interest in antiques, and family life. When I congratulated him on his successes, he responded with humility, something he had gained since his youth. He had matured incredibly and changed immensely, but at the core, he was the same man with a love for the sport of cycling, fierce competitiveness, and drive that has made him one of the best cyclists of all time.   ❄

CHAPTER FOURTEEN

THE TEAM DYNAMIC

In the mid-1980s, a criterium was held in the heart of downtown Toronto. It was a race I had been looking forward to in the preceding months because many of my heroes were going to be racing in it. The race was the one event on the Canadian calendar where we would get a chance to see, in person and racing, the stars we read about in the foreign cycling magazines.

I still have a hat somewhere in the basement of my parents' home that has about 20 autographs scrawled on it from many of the greatest cyclists in the sport of that era: Guiseppe Saronni, Andy Hampsten, Steve Bauer. I had that hat pinned on the wall beside my bed for years. I can still remember getting flutters of excitement while riding our bikes downtown to watch the races. It was a highlight of my summer.

At the races now we are often asked to sign hats, posters, bottles, shirts, and even bare arms. When a little kid comes up to me, I often think back to my childhood days when I would go to the races to collect the autographs. I cherished those signatures for months, and the images of the riders fueled my dreams as I rode in the city parks.

Cycling is the most accessible sport for the public to watch and be in close proximity to the stars. Bike races come to different towns and cities, and rarely do people have to travel far to see the champion of the past year's Tour de France. How often does David Beckham kick around a soccer ball in Waregem, Belgium?

> FANS CAN TOUCH LANCE BEFORE HE HEADS TO THE START LINE, PUSH HIM WHILE HE CLIMBS THE ALPS, OR SHAKE HIS HAND AT THE HOTEL AT NIGHT. HE IS FAR MORE ACCESSIBLE THAN MOST OTHER SPORTS' HEROES.

Fans and media gather around our team bus at each race, but the media surrounding the team is increased tenfold when Lance is racing. The bus becomes a sanctuary from the crunch of the media outside its doors. Fans line up for hours in hotel lobbies waiting for a photo with or an autograph from with Lance. He signs countless copies of his books at races and poses for as many photos. Fans can touch Lance before he heads to the start line, push him while he climbs the Alps, or shake his hand at the hotel at night. He is far more accessible than most other sports' heroes.

Lance brings a completely different status to an event when he arrives. The media covers his every move each day and splashes images of him throughout the world. When I race with Lance, the Canadian media is far more aware that I am racing in Europe and takes great interest in the races we are competing in. The races that are the best to compete in are those with the biggest crowds. A big crowd makes it all that much more worthwhile and the pedaling a bit less painful.

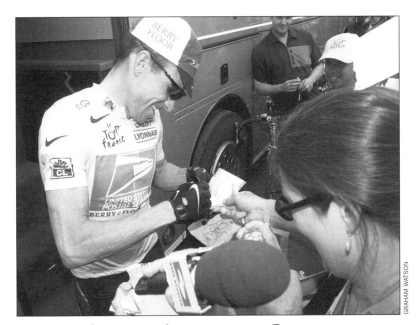

IN DEMAND: *Lance signs one of many autographs at the Tour.*

Not only does Lance take time to be available to the racing public, but he also devotes a lot of time inspiring millions of cancer
patients around the world. Sometimes at the races you'll see a few
folks struggling with cancer, and it is moving to witness how much he
has motivated them to fight for their lives. I imagine that many are not
cycling fans by origin but they have become interested in the sport
because it is what their hero does for a living and is his passion.

In addition, in Europe there are always a few vultures circling
around the hotels, buses, and start lines. They come with handfuls of
team cards, asking us to sign five or ten of them, and then they often
turn around and sell them for profit at shows and swap meets. Some
are true fans, but others are aggressive and self-serving, so it can get
tiresome seeing them at every race pushing others out of the way.

Our team also produces very few photo cards compared to other teams, making the U.S. Postal team photos more sought after by collectors. I am curious how much a 1999 signed Lance Armstrong card now goes for on the Belgian market.

Now that I am racing in the professional peloton and can see things from the inside, I realize that my view of the life of a cyclist has changed. There are certain things I still get excited about while racing as a pro and others I have perhaps started to take for granted. The things I thought were incredible when I was a kid, the things I dreamed about, are not really the same things I get excited about now.

As a child, when I received a water bottle, hat, poster, or any official team paraphernalia, that item was cherished. After having been professional for so many years and becoming accustomed to receiving suitcases full of team clothing, signing thousands of team posters, and tossing water bottles each day to the crowd, I have lost some of the appreciation I once had for the material items. Now my pleasures in the sport are different. I enjoy the feeling of having completed a good race, and then sitting with the team and enjoying a beer, talking about the day and the coming races. I realize, too, that what is most admirable is not a rider's *palmarès*, or results, but his qualities as a cyclist.

I race and train each day with many of the world's best athletes, and many are good friends. I have respect for riders in the peloton, but I no longer put any of them on a pedestal, because I have learned we are all human and in spite of our many accomplishments, we have faults like everyone else.

However, I still get excited when I see a heroic ride—the athlete who can dig to great depths and put forth a superhuman effort still inspires me. It excites me when I see Lance attack his rival Jan Ullrich like he is standing still on a mountain pass or when sprint ace Alessandro Petacchi comes off his teammate's wheel in the final meters, steps on the gas, and with a turbo kick blows everyone away. These are thrilling moments. But I realize now that the cyclist who wins is not always the most heroic or the one who has put forth the most impressive ride. Often it is the riders who

> *I REALIZE NOW THAT THE CYCLIST WHO WINS IS NOT ALWAYS THE MOST HEROIC OR THE ONE WHO HAS PUT FORTH THE MOST IMPRESSIVE RIDE.*

are not on television or not given accolades who are the strongest. Sometimes it is the *domestiques* who ride on the front for hours, or pull impressively fast over a climb, demolishing the peloton. At other times, it is the rider who crashes and then fights back from the accident, shorts ripped and bloody flesh exposed, to finish in the front group or pull for his teammates for a while longer. These are the riders and exploits that are often discussed on the way home in the team bus.

A rider who sits on a breakaway all day and wins the race does not necessarily impress the riders in the peloton, even if the newspapers the following day may have his photo across the front, and his victory may have looked impressive on television.

There are certain riders who, regardless of what team they ride for, everybody in the group is happy to see win a race. Frequently those riders are workhorses—always at the front struggling for their teammates but never winning. Cycling is a sport for which it is essential to have a strong team in order to win a race, but the team doesn't get the same accolades the winner does. There are champions, and there are the *domestiques*. Solid team efforts can achieve great things and create an incredible ambiance.

I have always felt that being a part of the winning team effort is better than a solo victory, because you have teammates to share the experience with. In the 2003 Vuelta a España, the team worked for three weeks to put Roberto Heras in a position to win the race, and it was not until the second-to-last day that he took the lead. But the sensation when he came through and won the race was felt by the whole group. The team was buzzing, and the fans were there to emphasize the feat.

The team time trial is the event where the whole team celebrates a victory together. Winning is a great feeling because everyone has struggled together for a common goal. In the Tour de France, the team members empty themselves daily for Lance so that he will win the overall title. But when they win the team time trial, they *all* get to kiss the podium girls and throw the flowers to the crowd. It is the one race where each cyclist is rewarded equally for his work.

In the Vuelta a Cataluña in 2002, we won the TTT, which opened the weeklong race and set up Roberto Heras for his eventual overall victory. On the podium we were ecstatic—we were the second team on the U.S. Postal roster, as the team racing in the Dauphiné Libéré a week earlier was considered the first team, and we had beaten the best in the sport. On the podium Christian doused the team and the press with champagne and completely soaked the podium girls, who were not too impressed because they had to go behind the podium to reapply their makeup.

When the radio earpiece is screeching that the team is leading and that we'll win, it sends shivers through my body. I can't feel the lactic acid anymore, and I can keep pushing with all I have until the line is crossed. In that experience, the adrenaline rushing through my body is intense, and not until it is all over do I realize how hard I was pushing. Once the line is crossed, the fans come into focus, the surroundings are realized, and sweat begins to ooze out of every pore.

Except for every four years when we compete at the Olympics, the world championship is the single event in the season in which we all race in our national team colors. The race draws out the patriotism in the fans as well: gone are the banners cheering on U.S. Postal, and instead you see flags of the different nations competing in the races.

In June 1991, in the center of Québec City, I put on my first national team jersey for the opening criterium of a stage race called the Grand Prix Mennen. We were all given one set of shorts and a jersey. As I pinned on my numbers I could feel flutters in my stomach, nerves of excitement. I was a junior racing with the seniors and professionals, and it would be a selection race for us for the world championships in Colorado Springs. I was 15 years old.

The start line was on the Plains of Abraham, a historic battlefield in which the French were defeated by the British—an outcome that has since influenced much of Canadian culture, policy, and politics. I felt proud to have the Canadian maple leaf on my back, but also felt like I had all the eyes of the spectators on me. I wanted to perform for my parents, for myself, but mostly for the jersey on my back and what it stood for.

In 2004, at the world championships, as in past seasons, I was again handed my clothing for the race. The same thoughts tumbled in my head. My friends, parents, and the Canadian fans were at the race to cheer me on, to support the Canadians, and to wave our flag. My name was painted across the road on the course, in Canadian colors, and a crowd of fans, in red and white, waving flags, cheered, and in true Canadian style, pounded hockey game chants out on the barriers. Each time I climbed the hill, saw my name on the road, and heard the cheers of the crowd a wave of inspiration and motivation coursed through me.

But with eight laps to go, I crashed and was forced to abandon the race. I tried to continue but the injuries made it hard to pedal and push. As I sat in a pizzeria with Dede and watched the rest of the race, I felt disappointed. I was broken inside because I had lost an opportunity, but more than anything else, I felt that I had let down the fans that had painted the roads and cheered me on for hours. I felt empty, sitting in a roadside café and watching the race I wanted desperately to complete. During the Vuelta, we raced on open roads without a spectator in sight for miles and only a few television cameras covering our progress, and that was an empty feeling. On a circuit lined with people, I feel a sense of motivation and purpose—we are there to put on a show.

Only one rider from each country gets to experience racing in the national champion's jersey each season. That jersey is different from a national team jersey, and it is worn year-round in every race the champion competes in. In a peloton filled with corporate logos and colors, the national champion represents his country by carrying the flag on his back. The jersey distinguishes him from his teammates and all of the other riders in the peloton.

In 2002 when we were racing in Spain, Dave Zabriskie asked Chechu why one of the riders in the peloton had red and yellow clothing, bike, and helmet. Chechu, who is normally quiet, considerate, and soft-spoken, was offended and said, "That is the Spanish flag, bitch, and he is the *national champion.*"

At the world championships in 2004, I was sad to see the U.S. cyclists enduring abuse from spectators because of their government's policies. On the course there was only one U.S. flag to be seen around the entire circuit, and peace signs and anti-Bush signs were painted prominently on the roads we raced over. Antiwar protesters harassed the U.S. team before the start of the race as they were sitting in their team cabins alongside the course, and this created a feeling of unease for some of the riders.

Fashions in the peloton parallel many of those we see in Western society, since trends that develop within teams eventually infect the entire peloton.

As a young teenager, I analyzed the pictures of the European pros and carefully imitated their styles and their positions on the bike. We raced up and down the hills of southern Ontario, the sounds of John Tesh's "Tour de France" theme repeating in our heads, and our hats perched just like Laurent Fignon or Dutch-climbing ace Gert-Jan Theunisse had worn theirs the previous week at the Tour. I would save my allowance and prize money for the latest Oakley sunglasses, and then wear them everywhere I went.

Why Do We Do It?

BY GEORGE HINCAPIE

Sometimes, teamwork means putting team goals ahead of personal goals. A lot of people ask me why I continue to ride for Postal when I could get more personal results on my own. What they don't understand is that I have had the chance to be part of history and help Lance win a record six Tours. I have been an important member of the world's most successful team and that is very satisfying to me. Winning a record six Tours is a greater achievement than any personal victory I could ever gain on my own. But trying to explain that to people isn't easy—there just aren't enough words to explain what it's like to be there, climbing off the bus, and starting the final stage to Paris alongside the yellow jersey.

All this success doesn't come easy. You have to persevere through the hard times in order to be a true champion. The 2003 Tour was very difficult for our team. We had won four Tours and were looking to win our fifth in a row. We knew what we had to do, but we still had to execute. Everyone doubted that we could do it. The race was really close for the entire three weeks.

After I finished the first individual time trial, I waited by the bus, by the finish line, and watched Lance on the big-screen TV. He was suffering; you could see it in his face. When you ride with your teammates as much as we do, you get to know what they look like when they're feeling good and when they're feeling bad. Lance looked terrible. You could see the pain on his face. His time splits were not as good as they should have been. He was losing time to his main rivals and the situation was dangerous. His lead was in jeopardy and we all knew it. He knew it. But he didn't quit. He did not give up. He dug deep and persevered through the hardest time of his Tour. He looked terrible at the finish. He was dehydrated and extremely tired. The stage could have crushed him and erased his entire lead, but he summoned up the energy to push himself to his physical limit. He persevered like a true champion to limit his losses and finish as strong as he could.

The next day everyone on the team was affected by Lance's effort. Morale was down as we sat by the stage start in the bus. I knew Lance needed some major support and I knew that he probably never realized just how inspiring he had been to the team and to me by persevering through that difficult time. That morning before the start, I pulled Lance aside and told him what I thought. I looked him straight in the eye and said that I have never been more impressed with his riding than I had been the day before. He was floored. I mean, here's this guy who has inspired us all, and he was truly touched. He couldn't believe that I was impressed with his riding on a day when he struggled so much. He was truly inspiring to all of us—even as we sat in the bus after that rough stage. That was just the pick-me-up he needed to regain his focus. We went on to win our fifth straight Tour de France.

In 2004, hairstyles flashed back to the 1980s; hockey hairdos were in style, as locks of hair rolled out from under helmets. In the late '80s, ponytails were the style in the peloton; everyone had one, and if a biker opted not to adopt that style, he simply let his long hair flow in the breeze, the top covered by a cycling cap sitting high on the head. Currently the caps are worn backward and low with the peak flipped up. When Eddy Merckx was winning the Tour, the cap was worn forward with the peak flipped up.

Lance has brought high socks and long shorts into style in the peloton. His tastes are more conservative; function and efficiency are more important than looks and style. Our team shorts are cut long, the socks are cut high—which are comfortable but not ideal for out-of-uniform tan lines. Our bikes are the fastest and some of the lightest on the market, but they are subdued in color. The style of our team uniforms was quite subdued and conservative as well, but with bright red stripes made specifically to stand out in photographs and on television, they provide an effective advertising billboard.

In the 2003 Tour de France, George Hincapie wore a black Oakley sweatband on his forearm; soon after, juniors throughout the world were sporting the same style.

The Italians are renowned for bringing flair into the peloton. Their kits are usually unique, standing out with bright colors and crazy designs. Mario Cippolini has been the Italian trendsetter during the past decade, although Marco Pantani had brought in the bandanna worn around his head. Super Mario always turns heads at the races, since he usually shows up at each race with a little something different to sport; a few times he's shown up in the buff with his shirt off or modeled nude on his bike. The media and housewives all over Europe follow what Super Mario wears or what he chooses not to wear closely.

In the 2002 Vuelta while cruising in the *gruppetto* up a mountain, Big Mario took off his jersey while still in the race, scrunched it in a ball, and tucked it into his shorts; not a tan line was evident, and a rosary hung around his neck and swung back and forth as he climbed. That night at the hotel he came dressed in white from head to toe, wearing white Nikes with "Cipo" embroidered on the back. When the results were handed out he had been fined for not wearing his jersey, but that was the exception, not the rule. Mario no doubt has the most fines in the peloton for breaking the UCI's dress code.

The biggest trend in the peloton in 2004 has been the emergence of the yellow "Livestrong" wristbands, which appeared on the arm of nearly every cyclist in the Tour de France and the Olympic Games. In a campaign to raise funds for Lance's cancer foundation, Lance, with Nike, developed these bands and sold them for $1 apiece. By March 2005, the campaign had raised $30,000,000 for cancer research and support. Since nearly everyone has a link to cancer in his or her circle of family or friends, the armbands have been an enormous success. Both John Kerry and George Bush wore the bands as they campaigned through the summer, and everyone from track-and-field athletes to hip-hop artists are still seen wearing yellow bands.

CHAPTER FIFTEEN

LOATHING IN HAMBURG & TOURING IN DENMARK

The World Cup in Hamburg, the HEW Classics (named for the electric company sponsoring the race), is the first race back for many riders after the Tour de France. It is a hotly contested race through the city streets of Hamburg, and usually showcases Germany's Tour de France superstars along with the other usual World Cup and one-day race hitters.

We arose before dawn, prior to our departure from the Brussels airport. The morning air was hot, sticky, and smoggy from city traffic pollution. My legs ached from the previous day's final stage of the five-day Région Wallonne race, and my mind was not yet focused on the World Cup that we were leaving for that day. The hotel breakfast buffet had just opened—plates piled with croissants, sticky buns, and eggs were laid out, but all I could stomach that early was a cup of coffee. I burned my mouth and tongue as I tried to gulp it down quickly, and so by the second sip I was unable to taste a thing because of singed taste buds.

Two riders were still asleep when the shuttle was ready to roll to the airport. Laurenzo woke them up, and by the time they were down, the bus had gone and we were calling taxis to get a lift to the airport just 500 meters (1,640 feet) away.

We had a team of fresh legs for the races. All of us had just come off a five-week break from racing. We were able to take a few weeks easy and then build back up to race fitness. The first races back, the first pedal strokes in the peloton, are always a shock to the system after such a long break. The rhythm of a race is entirely different from training—the speeds are quicker and the accelerations acute.

A three-week stage race, or grand tour, is said to give a rider an extra gear—more power and a higher lactate threshold. The intensity of the race cannot be replaced by training. Even with motorpacing and massive workloads, nothing can replace racing for gaining strength. Riders who come off the Tour are much stronger than those coming out of a hard training block, and that makes the HEW Classics a Tour rider's race. Due to its proximity to the Tour on the calendar, the riders in front are usually the guys who have finished the Tour without digging too deep and are still motivated mentally.

The plane was packed, and the coffee had me buzzing, somehow keeping my sleepy mind from going into a deep slumber. Halfway through the flight, my stomach began to ache and even light sleep became impossible due to hunger.

The cart came by full of drinks but no food. The day after races, the metabolism in the body is still cranked from the previous days' efforts, and often I'll find that I eat and become hungry soon after.

We arrived at the hotel in Hamburg in the early afternoon. Rarely is it 30 degrees Celsius (86°F) in northern Germany, but it was that day. The hotel didn't have air conditioning, and when we entered our rooms it was like stepping into a black plastic shed on a hot day. I stripped to my boxers immediately and had beads of sweat forming a pond in my belly button as I rested on the bed. I jammed through the TV channels, found a music video, and closed my eyes.

Ten minutes later I was climbing into my cycling gear for an easy ride, the Lycra clinging to my sweaty skin as I tugged the shorts up. Recently we had been receiving a new set of jerseys and shorts for each race since the team was consistently adding new sponsors after the start of the season. Our new set had Discovery Channel and Williams Trading branded on the front; both were additions for the Tour and end of the year.

On a rest day, sandwiched between two race days, the training ride is essential but usually brief. In Hamburg, we got on our bikes and tooled along the seaside for an hour.

Since the start of the road trip to Région Wallonne, Hamburg, and the Tour of Denmark, I had been rooming with Dave Zabriskie. Dave has a wicked sense of humor, a good collection of music, and rolls all his clothes up and binds them with elastic bands. He is much neater than I am, keeping his suitcase in order with his rolls of clothing neatly piled next to his coffee bags and French press, toiletries, and shoes. Despite our organizational differences, we both go to bed at the same time and are generally compatible as roommates. It is hard to room with someone who is on an entirely different schedule, and the most challenging situation is perhaps bunking with a guy who has just come from America and is jet-lagged while the other is on European time.

As we returned from our ride, the other teams were all streaming into the hotel. When a bike race comes to town, it completely takes over. Parking lots are invaded with team trucks, buses, and cars; the rooms are filled with riders, and the city streets become clogged with fans. In Hamburg, the hotel can accommodate a dozen teams; it becomes a zoo. The lobby chairs are filled with autograph hunters searching for the riders' scrawls they are missing in their books. Team trucks that line the outside of the hotel have tentacles of hoses and wires plugged into the hotel, which power the washers, dryers, and fridges.

A dining room was set aside for those of us associated with the race. Come 8:00 p.m., the room was a hive of riders and staff shoveling back plates of pasta in preparation for the next day's 250 kilometers (155 miles).

Half of the dining hall was full of emaciated, tanned riders who had just come off the Tour de France. The pre-Tour/post-Tour difference is impressive: Oreo tan lines accentuate toothpick arms and washboard chests. Riders have paper-thin skin covering a road map of veins on their arms and legs. Some riders are still robust, while others are wasted from the three weeks of effort.

After the pre-race dinner, Dave and I got up from the table, our bellies bloated uncomfortably from dinner, and lined up for a spot on the elevator up to the room. Dave had commented when we rolled out for our earlier ride that French rider Laurent Brochard was perhaps one of his true idols in the peloton. We had seen Brochard stepping out of his team car in the hotel parking lot; he was dressed in civilian clothes—denim multicolored, patterned jeans accentuated with a few stylish rips and a matching button-down shirt, the collar covered up by his teased and feathered mullet.

As we boarded the elevator, Dave looked at Brochard next to him who was now in his team clothing, mullet in a ponytail with the top bit of his hair gelled and spiked, and said, "Broocchhe!" Brochard nodded, gave Dave a perplexed look, and stepped off the elevator.

The HEW Classic is one of the best-attended World Cups on the circuit. From a rider's standpoint it is the easiest World Cup, because there are few difficulties on the circuit and the peloton simply flies along en masse over the smoothly paved Germany streets. During the entire six-hour race, there are few areas where there are not fans cheering, blasting air horns, or twirling noisemakers.

The 2004 race was a bit different for us than in past years. Occasionally fans booed us, threw water, spat at our team car, and gave us the bird. The Tour had brought out a hatred for our team. In Hamburg, we were in the heart of T-Mobile territory, but never have I seen such an aggressive attitude against a team. And it seemed as though it was becoming infectious, because it had spread from the slopes of l'Alpe d'Huez to the Champs-Elysées to the port in Hamburg.

THE TOUR HAD BROUGHT HATRED FOR OUR TEAM. IN HAMBURG, WE WERE IN THE HEART OF T-MOBILE TERRITORY, BUT NEVER HAVE I SEEN SUCH AN AGGRESSIVE ATTITUDE AGAINST A TEAM.

Laurenzo was a bit scared driving the team car up the climbs among the masses of hissing fans. Often the cars will get jammed up on the ascents, and if the car comes to a stop and the drunken masses on the hill take over, they could damage the car.

After the Tour de France, the champions of July are paid start money to attend short city-center races, criteriums, throughout

Europe. The jersey winners of the Tour wear their Tour jerseys. The race brings the champions people watched for weeks on television to their city. The atmosphere is festive and the environment similar to a carnival.

While we were in Hamburg, Lance and George raced in a few criteriums in northern Europe city centers and also a two-man time trial. At one of the criteriums, the team car was broken into, and a drunken fan charged at Lance trying to injure him. As cyclists, we are vulnerable to attacks, even while we are racing. It is incredible to see the millions of fans who support cycling, but it's also hard to witness the few who are aggressive toward rival teams. Hopefully, the hooligan mentality that infects European football will not permeate cycling.

Once Lance finished racing the post-Tour European criterium circuit, he was on a plane to the United States, where he would finish out the season. He races infrequently after the Tour, if at all, and most of us do not see him again until training camp in January.

As soon as we had arrived at the Hamburg airport and were picked up by the staff, we began hearing discussions about contracts and the upcoming season. During the Tour, contracts are discussed, and in the two weeks following the Tour, most riders and staff sign for the coming season. It is a stressful period for everybody.

The Tour is a taxing three weeks for the staff and riders and they come out tired and eager to spend time with their families and friends at home. The season is only half over but the end still seems a long way off. There are still the World Cups, the Vuelta, and the shorter stage races to attend.

Rumors fly around the hotel in the summer heat; we read on the Internet who had signed with Discovery and heard whisperings in the peloton about which riders on the team would be leaving and which had signed. In fact, most of the riders on the team actually learned that the team had signed the Discovery Channel as a title sponsor on the Internet. Johan, who knew the sponsor, would only tell us that it was a very different sponsor, a cool sponsor, one that none of us would expect, and that it started with the letter "D."

The team management had been looking for a new sponsor for several months after the U.S. Postal Service had decided not to renew the contract, feeling it had already maximized its marketing opportunities through the sponsorship. The Discovery takeover was announced in June shortly before the Tour de France began. For the Tour, the Discovery logo was added to the jerseys in small print. The signing of Discovery was a relief to the riders on the team and to the peloton as it secured jobs for many riders for 2005.

Within the peloton, everybody keeps their lips sealed tight until they have signed on the line for fear they may lose what they already have. The riders who have had a great Tour are often less motivated to finish out the season. Most of the guys on our team who have done the Tour are squeezed dry from their efforts and can think of little other than sitting at the ice cream shop with their families or having a beer with their friends. But there are races to be raced, and few team members, other than Lance, have the luxury to end their year after the Tour.

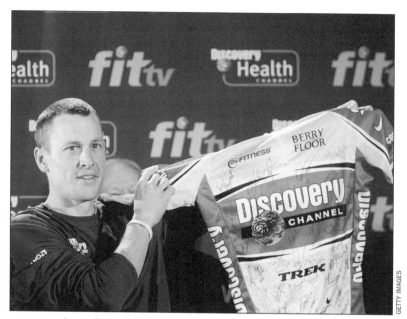

GETTY IMAGES

SIGN ON: *Lance Armstrong promotes his new team sponsor at a press conference.*

After Hamburg, we packed our bags and headed north to the Tour of Denmark. For many of us who did not race the Tour de France, we needed to participate in a big load of racing to prepare ourselves for races to come: the Olympics, the Zürich World Cup, and the Vuelta.

We arrived at the hotel in Denmark to more sunshine and high temperatures. I don't think the Danes have 30 degree Celsius (86°F) weather often, since none of the restaurants and hotels have air conditioning, and we were constantly sweating. It was difficult to keep hydrated when sweating profusely while we were resting or eating our meals in the hotel. At breakfast, a cup of coffee fired up my internal temperature, and I broke out in a full sweat in minutes; coffee is probably not the best beverage to have in the heat, but a morning cup is essential for me.

While the riders that did not race in the Tour were racing in Denmark, many of the riders that did compete in the Tour raced in the World Cup in San Sebastian, Spain, which is a tough race. The first three-quarters of the race are fairly flat, so the peloton simply cruises along at a steady speed. But in the last two hours of the race, the course becomes hilly, the pace picks up, and the selection occurs when the peloton hits the first ramps of the Jaizibel, a difficult climb that splits the field.

The San Sebastian World Cup is scheduled for a Saturday, unlike most other one-day races that occur on Sundays. In 2002, we were settled in the hotel on Friday night and waiting for dinner, and Ekimov was still absent. Eki had planned to drive to the start, and we began to wonder whether he was stranded on the road somewhere. Lance decided to send him a cell phone text message to ask him where he was. Eki responded with a short message saying he was getting ready for bed. Lance looked up from the cell phone puzzled and punched Eki's number in the phone to talk to him. Minutes later it was understood that he thought the race was on Sunday, and he was already in his pajamas getting ready to go to sleep. Eki lives at least four hours from San Sebastian in Tortosa. Realizing his mistake, he quickly packed his bags and drove through the driving rain to the hotel, arriving at 2:30 a.m. As always, Eki was strong and placed well in the race the next day.

In a two-week period we had raced 11 days and had pedaled many kilometers in three different countries: Belgium, Germany, and Denmark. For the riders who did not compete in the Tour de France, this had been a challenging block of racing and a tour of northern Europe.

After a five-week break from racing during the Tour, we all needed to get back into racing fitness and regain some intensity and speed.

The Tour of Denmark is a hotly contested race, and it was especially intense in 2004, since many riders were using the race to condition themselves for the coming Olympic races. The Danish tour is usually a battle in a crosswind and a race that favors the sprinters, and 2004 was not much different. We did, however, have one very challenging stage in the *bergs*, or small hills.

Denmark is the home turf of the CSC team, so roadsides and finish lines were splashed with red, black, and white jerseys and flags. The Tour of Denmark is an important objective for CSC, and the team arrived with a hit squad of in-form riders from the Tour de France, supported by several fast men for the sprints and to ride in the front in the wind.

In the first stage of the race, Australian Stuart O'Grady continued his winning streak from Hamburg and won the field sprint, grabbing the race leader's yellow jersey. From the first day to the finish in Copenhagen, the race was a battle between CSC and Cofidis—they shared five of six stage victories between them and also took the first three spots on the final podium.

The general classification in Denmark was decided on the third stage, where we were faced with a short but difficult morning road stage and then a short, flat evening time trial. Denmark is not known for its hills, but we pedaled over several that made the race intense and difficult; we started on tightly undulating and sinuous roads that shredded most of the field. The stage culminated with a very hard, short circuit that contained two climbs, one with a 21-percent gradient. At the end of the stage, riders were scattered over the course, and the overall classification was starting to take shape. Our team ran into a bit of bad luck when

Dave Zabriskie got a flat tire at the base of the climb. Max Van Heeswijk and I held strong in the second group and battled until the end, trying to bring back the breakaway that dangled 20 seconds in front of us.

Our goal going into the race was to place two riders in the top 10 and then try to win a stage. Max, the fastest sprinter on the team, was our best shot for a stage win. He finished in the top 10 daily but only really hit his stride the last stage. Unfortunately, he was boxed in and couldn't unleash his sprint.

The final two days of the race were intense and stressful due to a stiff wind coming off the Baltic. The race was constantly lined out, the peloton fracturing and then regrouping, nervous energy putting every rider and director constantly on edge. This style of racing can be very taxing—at day's end, I felt tired and depleted, not solely from the difficulty of the race but from the stress associated with racing in the wind and over small roads for 200 kilometers (124 miles).

The weather was beautiful and warm for the entire trip in Denmark, which is a bit abnormal. We were applying sunscreen, wearing our light jerseys, and sweating profusely in bed at night due to the lack of air conditioning in the hotels.

Between the morning and evening stages, we had five hours to put up our legs, eat a meal, and prepare ourselves for the individual time trial. The last rider off was at 8:30 p.m., so it would be a long day. The time trial went fairly well for us but was dominated by CSC, which placed five riders in the top 10. The outing was fair for our team, as we placed five in the top 20, with Victor finishing third. The two weeks of hard racing in the heat brought us all back into form, prepared us well for the Olympic Games, and built a foundation for the second half of the year.

CHAPTER SIXTEEN

THE 2004 OLYMPIC GAMES

The alarm sounded at 5:30 a.m. Antonio Cruz shook himself awake, opened the blinds to the already sunlit Danish skies, and slowly got dressed while I drifted in and out of a slumber. The previous evening we had finished racing at the Tour of Denmark. Shortly after the line had been crossed, the team had scattered in different directions: some to the airport, others to the airport hotel, and the staff in cars back to Belgium where the team's *services de courses* is located.

The *services de courses* is a warehouse where all of the team equipment is stored, from race bikes, spare bikes, clothing, and parts to the team trucks and cars. The warehouse is adjacent to a Ford dealership and repair center owned by Luc Verloo, our bus driver. Julien DeVriese runs the facility and spends many nights there as well. Among the buildings is a small house for the staff next to the warehouse, which has a few beds, a kitchen, a coffee machine, and everything they need to be comfortable for a few nights between the races when they can't get home.

Antonio had left on his flight by the time I was in the shower and preparing myself for the day's travel. The day after a stage race the body is in a bizarre state. I was feeling hungry and my legs ached slightly. My body wanted a rest but my mind wanted to keep going since I was feeling the rhythm during the previous week of racing.

In the lobby, a cup of coffee and a big buffet breakfast quieted the growl in my stomach. My bike was fetched from the hotel storage and I was soon boarding a plane for Athens. The Olympics were the next event on the schedule.

In 1996, I had raced the Olympic road race through the streets of Buckhead in Atlanta. Prior to the race in Atlanta, I was told by one of our national team coaches that he thought I could potentially complete half of the race. These were not motivating words for the biggest race of my life, but my teammate, Steve Bauer, quietly told me to be confident, that I would make it to the finish and could even be a part of the action in front.

I was young, 20, and had yet to start a race with the greatest cyclists in the world. I had read about them in the cycling media, lingered over photos of them climbing the alpine passes, but I had never had the chance to race with a world-class peloton.

The Olympic road race in Atlanta was the second time I had raced in the same peloton as Lance Armstrong, the first time being the previous year when he dominated the Tour of West Virginia. He was the favorite for the race in Atlanta, and started with a confident team around him.

The Atlanta road race was just after the final day of the Tour de France. Bjarne Riis, a Dane, had won the Tour and traveled after the finish to Atlanta for the Olympics. Steve Bauer was a good friend of the Danes, so we pulled up a few chairs beside them in the Athletes' Village dining hall one evening prior to the Olympic road race.

McDonald's sponsors the Olympics and so there are a few of their restaurants throughout the village. I have never seen so many fries and burgers consumed in one sitting as I did that evening watching the emaciated Danes from the Tour de France eat Big Mac upon Big Mac and large fries after large fries.

After picking up my bike and suitcase at the Athens airport, I was guided onto a bus that would drive us to the Athletes' Village. The mid-August heat beat down on the city bus as we drove the half-hour trip to the village. Prior to the Olympic Games, there had been a lot of discussion as to how the Games would unfold: would the Greeks have the venues, transportation, and security ready in time? Would the security be tight enough to hold off any terrorist attacks?

At the village the military presence was apparent: guards could be seen perched atop a few of the buildings, armed men guarded the gates, and security checks similar to those carried out at the airport were performed as we entered the village. But in comparison to Atlanta, the security didn't seem oppressive and the environment we entered at the village wasn't uncomfortable.

The bus was unloaded and I was in a full sweat due to the heat. Denmark had been hot, but now the light pants and T-shirt I had on were too much for the Athenian summer. From the bus I was ushered through the security screening to accreditation, where I was given a pass that would get me where I needed to eat, sleep, and compete.

I was in Athens to race in the road race, a race on a loop through the city streets in Athens. For road cyclists, the road race and time trial were the key events, although there were also track cycling events held in a striking velodrome designed by Spanish architect Santiago Calatrava, and a mountain bike race staged in the mountains close to the Athletes' Village. The Athletes' Village was just like a small town, with restaurants, laundry service, a movie theater, Internet cafés, a music store, a post office, a gift shop, a bank, and a hair salon.

After receiving my accreditation I was free to roam the village and get settled in my room. The village in Athens had just been finished, and the sod for the lawn was still being laid as I made my way to the Canadian sector. The village was divided into clusters of condos housing each nation. Flags adorned the buildings; maple leaves welcomed Canadians and kangaroos welcomed Australians across the street. Just down from our dorms were the dorms for the U.S. team where Dede was staying with the other American cyclists. The U.S. dorms stood out in sharp contrast to all the others in the village, because they were not decorated with flags but were stark white as a security measure.

We had quite a Girona contingent at Athens since Tyler Hamilton, Levi Leipheimer, George, Dede, and I were all there for the races. Although he'd made the team selection, Lance had declined his spot due to the stresses of winning the Tour.

Dede, who was in Athens to race in both the time trial and road race, had several Homeland Security agents staying in the room next door. Apparently, that room was the central command post for all of the

Olympic Village. In the U.S. dorm, there was also a central escape ladder allowing access to the roof, which I didn't see in any other building.

The Israeli dorms were different from the others as well, because they had no flags and there was security fencing wrapped around the building, which backed up to a military base on the north end of the village.

In addition to flags, some nations decorated the exterior of their dorms. The Aussies had life-size stuffed kangaroos, the Cubans had a portrait of Fidel Castro covering an entire side of one of the buildings, the New Zealanders had native Maori totems and sculptures, and the Brits had vintage red telephone booths and golf carts fashioned like London taxis and antique cars.

The cafeteria was a great place to people watch, as there was a constant stream of different body types passing by. It was fun to guess which sport each athlete competed in: some stood out, like the gymnasts, shot put, and discus throwers, and certain basketball stars, like Yao Ming of China.

With more than 10,000 athletes and team staff staying in the village, and a dining hall seating over 5,000 people, the village was busy with bikes, pedestrians, and buses. The cyclists usually opted to move around the village on their bikes because we're not great walkers and have the advantage of having our bikes close at hand. The Dutch Olympic team was supplied with hundreds of orange Giant cruiser bikes, so that their athletes could run about the village without being on their feet too long. Prior to the road race and time trials, the

dining hall entrance was crammed with race bikes, ready for the following day's race with frame numbers and race wheels.

The other option of transport was to take a city bus. The buses were
empty the first days of the Olympics but completely crammed with athletes as we entered the first week of competition. There was a stark contrast between the buses that run through the streets of North America
and the buses that cruised through the village. These buses were city
buses but brand-new, clean, without graffiti saying "Spiros loves Voula"
on the backs of the seats. Piled in the bus were lean, healthy, laughing
individuals as opposed to stressed, overweight commuters dreading a
day of work. Somber suits were replaced with comfortable athletic wear
brandishing flags and flashing bright colors.

The dining hall contained a world of options: flavors and dishes to
suit the diversity of the village. In addition to the main dining hall in
the village, a second smaller dining hall could accommodate a couple
hundred athletes comfortably.

Gymnasts ate small plates of food and nibbled away while the
basketball players, weight lifters, and wrestlers shoveled in plate after
plate of food to fuel their engines for their competitions.

Athens was George Hincapie's fourth Olympics. He started his
Olympic career in 1992 in Barcelona as a first-year amateur, fresh out of
the junior ranks and only 18. The Athens Olympics was the first time he
had stayed in an Olympic Village, since the U.S. team had always stayed
outside the village for logistical and training reasons in past Games.

As we strolled through the village after having just settled our
bags and bikes in our new rooms, we talked about being in the village.
In many ways it was a change for us; on the road with U.S. Postal we
sleep in nice hotels, eat at restaurants, and show up to the races with

crowds of people waiting for autographs. At the village we were just a bunch of athletes eating off a buffet, sleeping in dorms, and waiting in line to get in the village, go through the security check, or pile onto the bus to get to the laundry facility.

It was fascinating to eat with athletes whom nations idolize, athletes who are paid immense sums to wear a certain deodorant, athletes who made history just prior to eating a Greek kabob off a plastic tray in the dining hall. It was remarkable to see all the athletes, no matter what their income levels or achievements, living in identical accommodations.

I arrived in Athens on Monday, August 9, and the cycling road race was not until Saturday, August 14. I had to train for a few days, recover, and get ready for the race. As I had just completed a two-week block of racing, I didn't need to do much hard training, but I did need to keep my body moving and comfortable on the bike.

A training circuit had been set up outside the village for the cyclists to cruise around safely while in Athens. Since the village was located about 15 kilometers (9.5 miles) from the city, the roads surrounding the village were away from the buzz of traffic and quite scenic. The racecourse was about a 45-minute ride from the village and secluded in the hills.

IT WAS FASCINATING TO EAT WITH ATHLETES WHOM NATIONS IDOLIZE, ATHLETES WHO ARE PAID IMMENSE SUMS TO WEAR A CERTAIN DEODORANT, ATHLETES WHO MADE HISTORY JUST PRIOR TO EATING A GREEK KABOB OFF A PLASTIC TRAY IN THE DINING HALL.

While training on the course the first day, we noticed signs posted stating photos were forbidden. Off in the distance we could see military trucks and buildings, but the area didn't really look as though there was much up there that was top secret.

As the week passed, more military personnel were sitting along the course that was marked out for us. Armed guards sat in the bushes eating sandwiches while others perched on boulders sipping water. Eric Wohlberg, my Canadian teammate, had been riding the course twice a day, morning and evening, and had become familiar with the environment around the circuit. Behind a cluster of trees, Eric noticed a surface-to-air missile on a truck and made us aware of it. The security on the track clearly wasn't for our protection.

A couple of days prior to the race, the media began following teams while training. As the Russians left the village, a camera crew accompanied them up to the course to film them training together before the Olympic showdown. When the team arrived at the course, the camera crew took their lens off of the team and started to film the helicopters and missiles in the distance. The guards saw them filming, pulled them over, arrested the crew and held them at the roadside for half a day with the Russian team coach. The guards went through the film and photos and deleted all that had been shot while up on the circuit.

Ekimov was part of the Russian team and was the reigning Olympic time trial champion from the 2000 Sydney Olympics. The Olympics had been his goal for the past four years. Eki has had a fantastic track record in the Olympics, winning gold in 1988 and 2000. In Athens, at 38 years old, he beat the odds and won another medal in the individual time trial—not gold this time, as Tyler Hamilton edged him out, but he was a close second.

Unfortunately for us, the road race was scheduled for the first day of the Olympics, which eliminated the cyclists' hopes to attend the opening ceremonies. The ceremonies are a long evening and the athletes usually spend several hours on their feet, marching in and around the stadium, which is not the best thing for the legs the day before a race. And with the heat being so extreme in Athens, it was not a good idea to chance getting dehydrated the night before the race either. We saw a bit of the ceremonies on television and then went to bed.

We drove to the start of the road race from the village in a motorcade of team

CASEY B. GIBSON

OLD WARRIOR: *Ekimov fights his way to a silver medal at the '04 Olympic Games.*

cars and coaches; police on motorcycles closed the road, and a lane on the highway had been designated for Olympic teams and personnel. Traffic in Athens was a concern prior to the Games, but summer vacation had liberated the usually congested roads of local cars and delivery trucks in time for the Olympics.

At the start/finish area we settled ourselves in the foyer of a department store, away from the oppressive heat, to prepare ourselves and get ready for the race. With U.S. Postal, we have our team bus at the start and don't need to think about finding a comfortable spot to sit down, get changed, and pin our numbers on. The following day Dede and her American teammates took over the second floor of a Starbucks to get ready for the race. They had their gear laid out all over the tables and chairs and did their radio checks over cups of coffee.

It was unusual seeing Jan Ullrich, one of the great heroes of cycling and the 2000 Olympic road race gold medalist, unpacking his bag while sitting on a curb in the heart of the city. The German team of superstars sat alongside him and prepared quietly for the race.

The course wound through the streets of downtown Athens, past the Acropolis and other historic sites that draw tourists to Greece each year. There were no big difficulties on the circuit, but there were no easy sections either for relaxing and recovery. From the climb to cobbles to corners, it was a relentless circuit.

We knew that the heat would be another factor making the race difficult. Racing 240 kilometers (149 miles) in the middle of a hot summer day is hard on the body. Prior to the start I loaded my pockets with hydration salts, Clif Bars and Gels, and drank as much as possible. The race followed a pattern similar to a World Cup competition—we pedaled at a mellow pace in the first couple of hours and an early breakaway took off. Magnus Bäckstedt, a Swede, did almost half of the race solo. Magnus is a brute of a man, the tallest and largest in the peloton, weighing in at just under 200 pounds. He won the 2004 Paris-Roubaix, the biggest win of a career that has also been highlighted by a Tour de France stage victory.

There were six U.S. Postal riders in the race, and we were all riding for different teams: George, Eki, Benoit, Max, Victor Hugo Peña, and me. Vince Gee, the U.S. Postal mechanic, serviced the American riders in Athens as well. Gone were our Postal team clothes. We each wore the colors of our respective countries. It was unusual seeing all the guys I spend so much time with during the season out of their usual gear. The different uniforms made it hard to recognize riders as they attacked or moved around in the peloton.

In the last laps of the race, I felt like we had entered a sauna. In the peloton I could see the effect the oppressive heat was having on the riders; everybody looked tired and unmotivated. Attacks were made but they were nowhere near as potent as they would have been in cooler temperatures.

My goal going into the race was similar to that at the 2003 world championships in Canada: race with every ounce of energy I had left, attack in the final, and try for a medal. With 7 kilometers to go (4.5 miles) I attacked when the peloton came to a standstill. I gained a solid advantage on the field and was in pursuit of a bronze medal; Paolo Bettini and Sergio Paulinho had already jumped away the previous lap and were sure to finish first and second. As I pushed on the pedals out front, my legs began to cramp, then my stomach muscles. Axel Merckx, who eventually finished third, had attacked the peloton as well, and came up on me at quite a speed. I put my head down and tried to keep his pace, but my legs were cramping and it was over. With just over one kilometer to go, a charging peloton caught me, led by German Jan Ullrich. I tried but had come undone when it counted. As I crossed the line and stopped pedaling, my legs seized up with cramps.

After the finish line, riders were laid out on the ground while others held themselves up resting their torsos on their handlebars. Everybody looked weak. We climbed back in the cars and headed to the village. A shower and a cold drink was all I desired.

I left the Olympic Village the day after Dede's road race, because the World Cup in Zürich was coming up the following weekend and I needed to get home, train, and be settled before traveling to another race. I had to admit that I looked forward to being in my own bed again after the excitement and chaos that surrounds the Olympics. I would have loved to have stayed in Greece, watched some other events, and visited the islands, but there were still races to be ridden and half a season to complete. But returning home meant I would miss Dede's time trial. She had won or placed well in nearly every time trial she had competed in during the season, so in my mind she was a favorite for a medal.

As Dede raced out of the start house, I bit my nails and watched the televised broadcast at our apartment in Girona. I have raced thousands of races and never get too nervous myself anymore. But when I watch Dede race, I have a hard time calming my nerves and I look away from the television constantly, trying to multitask to take the edge off.

As she neared the first time check, I was sitting on the edge of my seat, my fists clenched tightly. The first time check said she was leading the race. I didn't sit down again, and paced throughout the apartment for the next 20 minutes.

At the end of the day, three Americans had medaled: Tyler Hamilton took gold, Bobby Julich had a bronze, and Dede got a silver. It was a good day for America, and two of the three medals could be shared with our friends in Girona.

Dede's medal in Athens had me motivated as I boarded the plane two days later to the Championship of Zürich. In the lead up to the race, Italians and archrivals Paolo Bettini and Davide Rebellin had done some serious racing—especially Bettini, because he had won the Olympic gold medal on top of racing the two World Cups, San Sebastian and Hamburg. Both riders were vying for the overall in the season-long World Cup series and both were on form to win in Zürich.

SILVER LINING: *Dede Demet Barry pedals for her medal during the Olympic time trial.*

The Championship of Zürich was the last of the World Cups until the two final weekends in October: Paris-Tours and Tour of the Lombardy. Rebellin and Bettini had been dueling for the lead of the World Cup since the start of the year, but Bettini was slowly tugging Rebellin's leader's jersey from his shoulders, placing ahead of him consistently in the latter races of the season.

Zürich is a tough race, with one large, rolling loop and then four hilly 40-kilometer loops. The final loops are relentless, with corners, false flats, a hard, long climb, a shorter, steeper climb, and a flat section open to the wind along the lake as the course nears the finish.

As George and I neared the dining hall for breakfast the morning of the race, Dave Zabriskie headed up to the room, already having eaten his pre–World Cup feast of eggs, rice, bread, and cereal. Usually we eat about three hours before a race to let the food digest so that we're not on the start line feeling bloated. Dave had fueled up early and was motivated for the day ahead. His goal was an early breakaway, and he tried to rally a few troops for his escapade as we rolled up to the start line. Nobody seemed too interested in flogging themselves off the front for 200 kilometers with him, but after the race started he soon found himself out front with another young rider from the Liberty Seguros team.

CASEY B. GIBSON

Dave has a huge motor and turns out solid performances in time trials. In the last few years he has had some horrible crashes and is therefore, understandably, scared of the bunch.

DECORATED CYCLISTS: *Americans Dede Demet Barry, Tyler Hamilton, and Bobby Julich show off their time trial medals.*

Let him loose out front and you may never see him again. We didn't see him on Sunday for five and a half hours. As soon as he was away, he hit the accelerator and the gap grew to an impressive 21 minutes.

Behind, the race ambled along slowly, in typical World Cup style, until we neared the final hours of the race. Then the pace slowly increased, the field shrinking with each climb.

Paolo Bettini wore a gold jersey and rode a bike with gold highlights to celebrate his victory in Athens the previous week. His form continued to be impressive; he fought off every challenge from Rebellin and also attacked aggressively several times on the climbs.

After Dave was caught, it was up to George, Triki, and me to battle in the front of the group and try to win the race. We had our opportunities and took them when we could, but to no avail. The race came down to a group sprint. It didn't really end the way we had hoped, because George was boxed in the group on the left side of the road while I followed with an acceleration on the right. We both ended up in the top 10, which was good but disappointing.

As soon as the race was over we had an alcohol towel shower in the camper, or *buske*, and were quickly packed into a car and raced toward the airport. We had less than an hour between the finish and the plane departure so it was touch and go as to whether we would make the flight. In a full sweat we checked in and raced to the gate only to be told the plane was broken and would be delayed. Four and a half hours later we were still at the gate, with only a couple of sandwiches in our stomachs and almost seven hours of racing in our legs. At that point, all I wanted was a shower and my bed. At 11 p.m. we were told the plane wouldn't be leaving until the next day, and so we should pick up our bags, head to a hotel, and get settled for the night—a long day only made longer. But all ended on a positive note, with a nice room, a long shower, and a big breakfast the next morning.

CHAPTER SEVENTEEN

LA VUELTA A ESPAÑA

We sat in a hotel in León, Spain, waiting for "the games" to begin. All the riders in the 2004 Vuelta a España had to be at the hotel three days before the start for medical testing, which essentially meant a blood test.

The 2004 Vuelta was to start out with some flatter stages as the race went across the middle of Spain toward the Mediterranean and the coastal town of Valencia. Valencia would host the first of three individual time trials, the next one up to the peak of the Sierra Nevada and the last as the final stage in Madrid.

We rode our time trial bikes in the days leading up to the start so we would get comfortable on them and get used to riding together in formation again as a team for the opening stage, a team time trial in León. Unlike the Tour de France team time trial, which is always about 64 kilometers (40 miles), the TTT in the Vuelta is very short, 22 kilometers (13 miles). In a short time trial, it is crucial to start out quickly because it is hard to regain time lost in such a short distance.

As soon as we get into formation on our aerodynamic time trial bikes, it is amazing how fast we can go with minimal effort; the combination of the formation we ride in and the bikes we ride is so efficient it gets us rolling really fast.

With several flat stages in the first week of the race, we planned to ride for Max and set him up for field sprints. The wind would be a big factor as we headed across the center of the country. After the opening team time trial, splits in the peloton would be the only thing that could change the overall classification until we reached Valencia.

Our team approached the Vuelta with a more open team plan than we had used in past years when Roberto Heras was the team's clear overall classification threat. Both Floyd and Triki planned to race for the overall, but we didn't know how they would hold up over three weeks after having done so much work in the Tour for Lance. The decision was that they were to take it one day at a time and do the best they could. The rest of us were there to race for stages throughout the race, taking opportunities when possible, picking stages that suited our abilities. Without a distinct leader as we had in past years with Roberto, we instead had several cards to play, so it would be interesting to use a new team approach in this three-week stage race.

The second half of the race would present some vicious stages with altitude profiles that looked like the jaws of a wolf. Clearly the race would be exciting until the last kilometer was completed in Madrid. It was also evident that the general classification contenders would have to ride conservatively early in the race so they could save energy for the final week.

Dave Zabriskie had been doing well in time trials in the preceding month and seemed to be in great form for the start. "Briskie the kid," a nickname given to him by one of the guys on the team, was expected to finish well in the time trials at the Vuelta. In training he looked smooth and powerful and capable of doing well in a solo event.

Waiting around for a race to start is like sitting at a movie theater and waiting for the film to begin. We were in the hotel ready for the show without much to do but put our legs up and wait.

The 2004 Vuelta would begin with a team time trial. The TTT is one of my favorite events: it takes a complete team effort, and the feeling when everything is running smoothly is unparalleled by anything else in sport. During the effort, the whole team is completely focused—it feels as if we are riding in a tunnel with nothing but the open road in front of us and the voice of Johan encouraging us over the radio, the noise of the disc wheels, the sound of the wind and our breath blocking out all other distractions.

In the past two years, we had finished second in the Vuelta team time trial, both times due to a slow start. So our major goals for the first day were to start out quickly, get into our rhythm as quickly as possible, and stay on the speed until the finish.

The race was very technical at the start in León. We had to negotiate several roundabouts, corners, and speed bumps before we could focus on simply going as fast as possible without blowing up the team.

Floyd had a strong ride, taking long pulls and also motivating us all as we raced. He yelled at the top of his lungs a few times, "We can win this race, come on guys!" In the last meters when we knew we had won the stage, Johan told us to let Floyd cross the line first since he deserved the gold leader's jersey for his efforts.

Floyd was my roommate for the race and it was definitely inspiring seeing a gold jersey lying in his suitcase. It was also a thrill going to the podium with the whole team after the TTT and celebrating our achievement as a group. It is always a relief to get a race started on a good note, and it was a nice sensation to be on our way around Spain with Floyd in the yellow jersey.

Willy, the team chef, was unable to cook for us at the hotel in León because the hotel's insurance policy didn't allow him into the kitchen. I think he was looking forward to moving on from León as well, eager to practice his skills at the next hotel kitchen.

In the 2003 Vuelta, we had about 15 kilometers (9 miles) of easy riding in the entire three weeks of racing. The speed in 2003 had scared us all, so before the start in 2004 we were all thinking about that. But, in the first road stage of the 2004 Vuelta, we pedaled at a steady tempo for almost the whole day. The pace was relaxed enough that we could chat with other riders and not stress about being well positioned in the front. That is unusual for our team but nobody complained. Johan was silent on the radio, which was also unusual, staying true to his word and approaching the race in a more relaxed manner than in previous years.

The stage was an essentially flat 200-kilometer (124-mile) journey over to Burgos from León. We started in a fairly strong head wind, which in turn killed any ambition riders had for getting an early breakaway. We tooled along at a leisurely speed and progressively went faster as the finish approached. And we went fast toward the finish, as the average speed for the stage was around 42 kilometers per hour (26 mph).

Our main goal going into the second day was to keep the yellow jersey within the team and then perhaps, if Max felt good in the final section, we would help him out as we raced toward Burgos. To keep the jersey, we had to keep an eye on one of our two guys for the bonus time sprints; Telekom was the only team that could threaten the lead without a rider winning from a breakaway. If Erik Zabel won a time bonus and the stage, which was well within his capabilities, the jersey would be on his shoulders. Max won the first sprint and in doing so put himself in the gold jersey.

The day did not start well for me; I had a crash that left me bruised and with a few grazes. This happened early on in the stage, which in some ways was good because it allowed me to loosen up on the bike as the kilometers passed.

When a rider crashes, the first notion is to get up and get going again, and that is what I did as soon as I got my chain back on my bike. But I didn't look at my rear derailleur, which was bent and useless. Over the radio, Johan yelled at me to get off and wait; behind me the mechanic was chasing me on my spare bike, in his sneakers and jeans, with a set of spare wheels in his grasp. Soon enough, with Victor's help, I was back in the peloton, comfortable on my spare bike. Within 10 kilometers (6.2 miles) Johan came over the radio again to tell me that my race bike was fixed and that I could jump back on it again. Bikes are always a little different in feel and position, even if they measure and look identical. I hopped back on my primary bike and settled back into the race.

Several of us on the team had leader's jerseys in this stage for all the different classifications, since the organizers awarded all the jerseys on the first stage. Theoretically, Floyd should have had them all, because he crossed the line first in the team time trial. But because he was wearing the leader's jersey, I had the honor of wearing the points leader's jersey (a bright blue jersey with small fish all over it). The pattern looked somewhat like children's wallpaper or a pattern on children's pajamas. I received many comments in the peloton from the other riders about it, including, "It smells like fish around here." From what I understand, the sponsor was a fish food company.

The final kilometers ended up being very fast and sketchy, so Max decided not to take any chances and just rolled to the finish in the bunch. He climbed off his bike and onto the podium to put on the gold leader's jersey.

I arrived at the hotel and I was aching from the crash. My back was tight and sore from another rider's brake lever hitting my sit bone. The second half of the stage I found it hard to pedal with both legs—the pain on one side was more intense than the other.

After getting to the room I settled in with Guennadi Mikhailov, or Mika, who was my roommate for the night. Mika is a good roommate: he's quiet, but a conversationalist when he gets comfortable in an environment. He watches movies, reads Russian novels, and spends a few minutes each evening stretching.

Mika injured his back before he came to U.S. Postal in 2003, and when he arrived at our team his spine was completely crooked while sitting on his bike. On a bike it is crucial to be balanced and well positioned so that the rider can comfortably produce as much power as possible for hours. Mika's crooked position was not good and not productive. Two years later he was sitting straight and nicely aligned on the bike, his legs pumping up and down like pistons.

As we sat in the room together, he pulled out a rubber mat 3 feet in length with hundreds of short nails sticking through the rubber. He placed it on the bed, took off his shirt, and sat back on top of the short, pinlike nails. I looked over, puzzled, and asked what he was doing.

He explained that the nails were for relaxing his back muscles, and they helped his legs recover from the race as well. He had bought them from a doctor in Russia that had helped him with his back problems. He proceeded to say that he attributes the straightening of his back and position on the bike to the nails.

I was in pain, sitting on the bed icing my back, trying to decrease the inflammation. I asked if I could try the nails. I figured it could only help. After 10 minutes Mika had finished up and I placed it on my bed, relaxed, and eased myself onto the nails. At first it was painful, but after a minute or two my legs began to relax, my back relaxed, and the tension in my backside eased.

As I was on the nails, Dirk came in to pay us his nightly visit, to check up on us and see how we were feeling. He saw me on the nails and asked, "What's this?" Mika explained what the nails were for and Dirk asked if he could try them after I had finished. Dirk and Johan both have back troubles from their racing careers, pain that is aggravated by driving behind the race for hours each day. That night they both tried the nails and seemed impressed.

Because stage 2 was flat and slow, we expected stage 3 to have a vicious start with incessant attacks. That never happened, and we cruised along, building nervous tension due to the wind and anticipation of attacks for the first hour or so of racing. Then, the attacks finally started at a ferocious rate due to the built-up energy in the peloton.

We started the stage with the same tactic as the day before—to put riders in breakaways and to help Max out for the finish. Benoit Joachim jumped into the breakaway, the peloton slowed down, and the gap opened to 8 minutes. With the time bonuses on the road, Benny rode himself into the leader's jersey, a couple of seconds ahead of Max.

Having crashed the day before, I was feeling sore and achy all over. Thankfully the stage was tame, so I didn't have to inflict too much muscle damage and could give my body time to recover before we hit the hills at the end of the week. The jersey was still within the team. It had been shuffled around a little between a few of our guys, which was cool.

As we traveled through the center of Spain the roads tended to be long, flat, and open to the wind. Unlike the Tour de France, the Vuelta a España does not tend to attract huge crowds on the sides of the roads except for the critical mountain stages and when we race through the bigger cities. The arid desert landscape and lack of fans sometimes make these long, flat stages a little tedious, although they can also produce an exciting race when the wind blows.

On a bike, the biggest front chainring and the smallest rear cog combination produce the biggest gear ratio and, therefore, the gear in which you can travel at the highest speeds. A standard professional gear ratio is a 53-39 chainring combination on the front with an 11-21 cog combination in the rear. On mountain stages, the pros opt for smaller gears, installing 23 or 25 cogs in the back, and when there is a lot of descending or a finish on the downhill, they opt for a 54-55 or 56 in the front to make a bigger gear and travel at higher speeds.

On the stage 4 start line, I noticed that every team in the peloton had fitted either 54- or 55-tooth chainrings in anticipation of a super-fast stage with a big battle in the crosswind. At the end of the day, the battle never materialized; we were riding into a solid headwind for the majority of the 160 kilometers (100 miles) to Zaragoza. The big plates were not needed, and I don't think we even managed to get below the 13-tooth cog on the back because of the intense wind in our faces.

LEGENDS TRAVEL THROUGH THE PELOTON ABOUT PAST RACES INTO ZARAGOZA. A FEW YEARS BACK THEY AVERAGED JUST OVER 55 KILOMETERS PER HOUR (34 MPH) FOR 179 KILOMETERS.

We were riding down off a plateau, so much of the stage was slightly downhill. Legends travel through the peloton about past races into Zaragoza. The fastest road race on record was a stage to Zaragoza in 2001—they averaged just over 55 kilometers per hour (34 mph) for 179 kilometers. Our team didn't have the big rings fitted on our bikes back then, and after having worked hard to initialize the splits in the wind we were caught off guard and were dropped from the front group when ONCE came flying by, grinding out a monstrous pace in their 54 x 11 gears.

Cruising out of Soria at the start of stage 4, there was a strong scent of curry in the air in a town known for its herbal medicines and healing spas. I kept looking to see whether Matt White was ahead of me; he truly appreciates a good curry, and I thought he might be sweating it out from the previous night's dinner. Whitey came up to me during the stage and said he was craving Indian food. From what I could gather, the spice that gives curry its strong scent was growing in the fields we were racing alongside.

I think most of the peloton was relieved we didn't have to push and shove in the wind. I certainly was, because I needed as many easy days as possible to recover from my crash and heal. There was still a lot of nervous energy in the bunch, and that can become tiring, but it is nowhere near as tough as racing in echelons all day. Echelons occur when a crosswind is blowing at the peloton's side and causes it to fracture into smaller groups. Riders use each other to protect themselves from the wind, and in a race with strong winds the peloton will be in several groups that are lined across the road diagonally to get as much draft as possible. As the peloton is in pieces, each group is racing against the other with everybody trying to catch the one leading the charge.

It was strange to roll under the 20-kilometers-to-go banner at 27 kilometers per hour (17 mph). Usually, at that point in a race, we'd be racing at speeds between 50 and 60 kilometers per hour (31–37 mph). But I can attest to the fact that the guys on the front were working hard to go just 27 kilometers per hour—the wind was that strong. In the back, however, you barely needed to pedal, and could coast along comfortably in the draft.

There were quite a few crashes from the low speed and strong wind. The peloton would bunch up and then there would be abrupt stops due to gusts of wind, or riders on the front would decelerate quickly, resulting in one rider piling into another. Still, we were well into the first week of racing and Benoit was holding on to the golden jersey.

Stage 5 was both a good and a bad race for the team. We started out slowly again because of the wind, and pedaled along at 25 kilometers per hour (15 mph) for quite a while until a few attacks were launched. There were two potentially threatening breakaways, and thankfully we had riders representing us in both groups, meaning we didn't have to chase in the wind. It wasn't an easy day for the teams that spent time at the front chasing with their noses in the wind. For miles, we passed nothing but empty fields and dry grass.

The final portion of the stage was not hard enough to make any distinct selections but it was challenging enough to separate the climbers and general classification contenders from the rest of the peloton. The *gruppetto* (a large group of riders, usually *domestiques* who completed the work for their team early in the stage, not in contention for the overall or the stage win) was formed before the climb, since there was a crash on the road leading up to the climb. We all came to a stop in the road, and everybody behind the crash called it a day and then *gruppettos* were formed at the back.

The Telekom team lost several riders, and their Kazakh leader, Alexander Vinokourov, finished in the *gruppetto* because everyone on the team had come down with food poisoning from the last hotel. Vinokourov, or "Vino," is one of the most powerful and successful riders in the world, but he didn't have much luck in the race. Two days before the team fell ill, some idiot watching the race threw a cobblestone into the bunch just as we passed, hoping to witness a crash. Vino hit the large stone and broke both of his wheels. He was back in the bunch quickly but narrowly missed a serious injury. The police caught

the guy who threw the cobble and charged him. From what I understand he had a camera out, ready to film the crash that he hoped
would happen. This was another reminder that the cyclists in the peloton are truly at the mercy of the fans.

After the finish we all piled on the team bus to drive the 100 kilometers (62 miles) to the hotel. Soon after we had settled on the sofas,
smoke began billowing from the shower-kitchen area. The motor was
on fire. Luc, our bus driver, grabbed the extinguisher, got the fire under
control, and soon enough we were split up between the Telekom and
the Lampre team buses for the ride to the hotel. The Italian Lampre
team had a good setup inside their bus, with a two-spout coffee
machine, leather seats, a large lounge area, and a kitchen. When we
climbed aboard the Lampre bus 2003 world champion Igor Astarloa
was seated with his legs up on one of the seat backs. Igor is a friendly
rider and made us feel at home on their bus, constantly offering us
drinks, cookies, and fruit while making sure we had comfortable seating. In the last five years the Spanish have had two world champions:
Astarloa and Oscar Friere, and they are also two of the nicest, most
down-to-earth guys on the circuit.

By the time we got to the hotel, the report was that our bus was in
the midst of being repaired. The turbo had broken, and oil was pouring out of it onto the motor. We would get the bus back soon, they said,
but none of us put stock in that report. Luc and Pepe stayed in the bus
sleeping on the floor while repairmen worked through the night to get

it fixed. They couldn't move the bus off the mountain without repairing the engine, so they simply brought the new turbo up the mountain and did the repairs on the roadside.

During the stage, our two leaders had been up front, and Benoit made a valiant effort to maintain his jersey but lost it in the end to Triki. Things were looking good for the team as we looked forward to the coming stages. Everyone was still feeling good and I was praying I would be able to get over a cold and my sore muscles from the crash.

A week of racing had almost passed, we were in Valencia on the Mediterranean, and the team had held on to the gold leader's jersey for the entire week. Triki kept it for a couple of days, and with each passing moment in gold he became more of a Spanish hero. Ever since he took the lead, he grinned like a kid who had just found a full cookie jar.

The countryside became a little more interesting as the race turned south. We had gone from Alberta-like prairies to Southern California–like hills and orange groves, and from straight roads in the open wind to sinuous and undulating roads along the coast. The morale on the team was good and the leader's jersey was motivating us all. Up to this point, we had not really had to defend the jersey much at all. Having several riders in the top 10 put the team in a nice situation; we could put riders in breakaways and always have the leader on the road, forcing other teams to chase from behind.

As we raced toward Valencia near the end of the first week, it was clear from the start of the stage that the race would come down to a field sprint. From the first attacks in the first kilometers of the race we could see that the Fassa Bortolo team wanted to control the race and bring Alessandro Petacchi to the line for a massive group, or field sprint. He had dominated the field sprints since the start, so it was a safe bet that he would win in Valencia. And he did.

After most of the Telekom team went home sick, they had at least three staff to each rider. At dinner the team's rider table was virtually empty while the staff table was full with about 10 people on each side. The team would have been in trouble if their team leader, Cadel Evans, began to shine in the hills and needed a helping hand. Erik Zabel, their sprinter, didn't have many teammates left to help in the sprints either.

RACE LEADER: *Manuel Beltran is happy to be in the lead at the Vuelta.*

We had been without the team bus for a few days and it was getting uncomfortable preparing for each race day. Photographers crowded around the cars as Triki was getting changed into his yellow leader's jersey, and spectators peered into the van looking for hats, bottles, and autograph opportunities. Other luxuries we were struggling without were the coffee machine and the bus toilets. The port-a-potties at the race start were about 50 degrees Celsius (122°F) and baking in the sun. Nasty. We were pretty spoiled with our bus and we were certainly missing her. Luc reported that the engine was still in pieces but would be back together as soon as possible. I finally felt like I was starting to come out of the fog and funk that my cold and crash had put me in over the past few days. Stage racing wouldn't be what the doctor would prescribe for illness and injury, but I finally felt like I could pedal my bike properly again. I was hoping it was a trend.

In the individual time trial, we expected that Victor, Floyd, and Dave would ride well. It was a real surprise when Victor finished a close second to Tyler Hamilton, with Floyd and Triki in his wake, taking third and fourth.

Triki had one of the rides of his life in the time trial; he's not known as a time trialist but as a pure climber. After the race he said he was extremely nervous before the start, imagining all the cameras following him in the jersey, and he didn't want to disappoint the Spaniards watching the race on television or reading about it in the paper. Thoughts of failure gave him wings.

The terrain near Alicante was beautiful, with terraced olive groves on the mountainsides and orange groves in the valleys. From the start, the sun beat down on us, and within the first hour all of my clothes were soaked through with sweat. It was hard to race in the intense heat and keep hydrated. We were constantly downing bottles of energy drink and water, but I still felt dehydrated at the finish.

Things were beginning to shake up in the overall classification and the race was moving along nicely for us, with Floyd in gold and Triki in the top 10. After their incredible rides in the time trial, they managed to maintain their positions at the top of the classification. It had been an awesome ride for the team: we had won a stage and had held on to the leader's jersey since the start in León.

Morale within the team was still good even though Max decided to call it a race and left for home. He had been racing consistently at a high level since the Algarve in January, and mental and physical fatigue had finally caught up with him. He could no longer push himself at the red-line, so it was better that he go home and rest in hopes of winning some races later in the season.

We got our bus back, and it was a blessing. Luc said she wasn't rolling along quite like before, but she could get us to the start and home off the top of the mountain, which is essential. As usual, I was amazed at how he could maneuver the big vehicle through tight ancient towns or down the mountain roads. As we descended the switchbacks, the front corners of the bus would scrape the guardrails. It was dodgy, and I was glad I wasn't behind the wheel.

I think we had reached the point in the race where, if asked, we wouldn't have been able to remember all the stages or the towns where we had stayed. Dede says that 10 days into a race, I become pretty dull and quiet on the phone. It is strange being in a three-week race, because we are sort of in a bubble. The only contact we have with the outside world is through the news on TV, speaking with the staff of the hotel, or talking with family and friends on the phone. Otherwise, it is cycling all day, every day, for 21 days.

CHAPTER EIGHTEEN

A DAY IN SPAIN

A shaft of sunlight pierced through the crack in the curtains, waking me. The clock on the television said 9:10; my watch said 5 minutes after 9:00. I had 35 more minutes before I had to get up and start the day by filling my stomach with rice, eggs, and bread and go about getting my mind alert with a few cups of coffee. Thirty-five more minutes of sleep wasn't much, but it would be precious to my exhausted body.

Mornings during the Vuelta come late because the stages finish in the evenings. Ten more minutes of semiconscious sleep, and the phone rang. It was Dede calling from Girona. She had been up since 5 a.m., her mind already buzzing due to jet lag from her trip to race in San Francisco the previous week.

My mouth was dry and I chugged half a liter of water while she talked. She asked if I was paying attention to her. I told her I was, but I was still half asleep. While we conversed I threw on some pants, a shirt, and a baseball hat to cover my hair, which had gotten out of hand since the race began two weeks earlier. I hadn't even seen a hair salon, so the thought of getting it cut had only crossed my mind when I got out of the shower after the race and tried to comb out the knots. Yuri Kashirin, the Canadian team coach, told me not to cut my hair until the season's end because it would be bad luck. He said, "Like they do in the NHL play-offs." I hadn't heard a complaint from Johan regarding my messy hair, so I thought maybe I would hold off until after the world championships two weeks later.

My main concern at the time was getting healthy. My bedside was littered with tissues from a night of blowing my nose and coughing up phlegm. My nose was raw from all the sniffling and wiping. In the race I could just blow it, "farmer-style," but I tried not to scatter the germs on the other riders.

I stepped out of the room, still on the phone with Dede, and bumped into Johan who was vacating his room, bags in tow. We headed into the elevator and down to the breakfast room. Willy was dressed in his kitchen whites, scarf neatly tied around his neck, ready to cook up some eggs, whichever way we desired. I asked for an omelet, drank a glass of orange juice in one gulp, and poured a cup of coffee. The coffee served for breakfast at the hotels in Spain is mediocre at best. Usually it is instant, so I was plunging my own cups of coffee with a French press each morning, depleting the stocks of coffee that Floyd brings across from the States. Small things like good coffee make a big difference when you're into the third week of a three-week race.

I consumed two buns smothered in Nutella while I continued talking with Dede. She wasn't so happy that I was eating while talking to her. The omelet arrived, and down it went as well. It was good Willy was there with us, because he makes palatable food. At that point in the race, nothing much tasted good to me. I think we were all getting tired of eating. Fortunately, Willy was there to provide good pasta with a different flavored sauce each day. All of the other teams had been eating the hotel's limp, overcooked pasta.

Around the breakfast room, people associated with the race filled the tables and dug around at the buffet for the best croissant or a ripe piece of fruit to their liking.

Each day the race teams fill the local hotels. Team room lists are posted in the elevators like concert bills. Our team doesn't post room lists for safety reasons. Why a team would want the entire hotel, and anybody wandering through the lobby, to know where every-body is sleeping is beyond me. I think it simply is something that has been done forever and therefore it is still done.

> TEAM ROOM LISTS ARE POSTED IN THE HOTEL ELEVATORS LIKE CONCERT BILLS…. WHY A TEAM WOULD WANT THE ENTIRE HOTEL, AND ANYBODY WANDERING THROUGH THE LOBBY, TO KNOW WHERE EVERYBODY IS SLEEPING IS BEYOND ME.

Each night at the Vuelta, there are parties bumping throughout the city that attract everybody associated with the race except for the riders. Occasionally, rumors float through the peloton about riders sneaking out of their rooms to attend a party in town. We are intrigued and amazed by such stories because it is unimaginable to race after having a late night out.

Every race sponsor has a couple of women to promote their prod-ucts before the stage start and then again after the finish, as the riders are called to the podium and the champagne is sprayed. When the local hotels house the "podium girls," as they are called, the women draw the eyes of all the riders and staff who have been on the road away from their wives or girlfriends, as they mill around the buffets. It often seems as if there are as many podium girls around the race each day as there are riders.

Back in the room, I called Dede, and we chatted for a little longer. The room had a wireless Internet connection so I could catch up on my e-mail while I waited for our departure from the hotel. I look forward to reading messages from friends back home describing normal things: barbecues, group bike rides, dinner parties, or the weather. It takes me away from the race for a few minutes. In two weeks of racing, we have passed many historical sites, streamed by beaches crowded with tourists, and raced through lively cities. But we have seen none of it.

An hour in the room passed by as I stretched, pinned my numbers on, packed my bags, and got dressed to race. Richard came for the suitcases 15 minutes early again. The *soigneurs* show up for the cases each morning; they go to the next hotel in the mechanics' truck ahead of the race. Richard runs like a Swiss clock; well, actually faster because he is always early. I never unpack much so there isn't much to repack: a few casual T-shirts, a sweat suit, shorts, a couple of race jerseys, gloves, and socks is about it. Each evening after the race, one of the *soigneurs*, usually Alejandro, collects our dirty race clothes and regular clothing and throws them in the washer in the mechanics' truck. Basically, we can get through a three-week race with one jersey, a pair of shorts, and gloves, but they get a bit worn out after the halfway mark, so we switch them for new gear.

My suitcase was weighed down with a few magazines, *Harper's*, *The Walrus*, and *Vanity Fair*, along with my computer, the French coffee press, and a novel. Clothing aside, the only other thing is my toiletry kit, which usually includes a few different saddle-sore creams and soaps—one for especially bad saddle sores, the other for boils, and two antibacterial soaps for cleaning up after the race.

The race start today was only a couple of kilometers from the hotel, so to register we rode our bikes there instead of going in the bus. In front of the hotel, the buses and team cars lined up have drawn a crowd, and we are greeted and asked if we can pose for photos and sign autographs. I stepped over my bike, sat on the saddle, and pedaled to the start through the midmorning city traffic. My legs were still tender, but nowhere near as tender as my crotch.

It was easy to find the start because the organization clearly marked the directions from the hotel to the start with arrows posted at each intersection. When we arrived we went straight to the sign-in and then headed back to the bus, which had arrived from the hotel. Each morning we sign in on a piece of paper that sits up on a podium. It is a way for the announcer to introduce the riders in the race to the spectators, for everyone to recognize their heroes, and for the organization to also know who will not be starting the race.

From the sign-in, I rode back to the bus, signed a few autographs, and stood for photos on the way back. In the bus, bags were all over the seats and everyone was digging around for their race gear. The *soigneurs* had all the race food laid out ready for us to select. I opted for a handful of Clif Gels, since I couldn't seem to stomach solid food anymore. The race radios were laid beside the food, and we each grabbed our radio, plugged it in, and made sure it was working.

The coffee machine was grinding and sputtering out coffees while Johan tried to get our attention to call a pre-race meeting. Each day we have a short meeting before the race to discuss the tactics for the stage. On this particular day, we were trying to go in breakaways while Floyd and Triki followed, saving themselves for the final ascent up the mountain as they were placed well in the overall classification. The stage was tough and mountainous. We imagined that the Liberty Seguros team of race favorite Roberto Heras would control the race, so we didn't have too much to worry about. We just needed to stay near the front and avoid having to chase down any breakaways in which we were not represented.

After a short neutral start, where we were held back like cattle in a chute by the *commissaire*'s lead car, we were under way and attacks began immediately. From the start riders were yelling when others attacked, since they were tired and unmotivated to race. It had been a long season, and in a three-week race following months of racing, it is tough to remain motivated, especially for the non-Spanish riders who have been away from home most of the season. The Italians are the most vocal in the bunch, yelling *"gruppetto!"* at the bottom of the climbs, so that a steady group will form at the bottom to ride to the finish at a moderate pace, or yelling *"piano!"* when the pace is too fast in the *gruppetto*, or yelling at each other, or at people at the side of the road, or at their teammates over the radio.

> *THE ITALIANS ARE THE MOST VOCAL IN THE BUNCH, YELLING "GRUPPETTO!" AT THE BOTTOM OF THE CLIMBS . . . OR YELLING "PIANO!" WHEN THE PACE IS TOO FAST IN THE GRUPPETTO, OR YELLING AT EACH OTHER, OR AT PEOPLE AT THE SIDE OF THE ROAD, OR AT THEIR TEAMMATES OVER THE RADIO.*

After an hour of racing a few of us called the team car to get bottles of fluids. We filled our jersey pockets with drinks, and then raced back up to the front to hand bottles out to the team. Each rider on the team takes turns going back for bottles during the race, except, in this case, for Triki and Floyd since they were our leaders in the general classification. When picking up bottles from the team car, you can usually take a little push off of the bottle passed up by Johan, who was driving the car. The *commissaires* watch closely that the bottle is not held on to for too long, but they turn a blind eye if a bottle is held on to for just a few seconds. A little push is welcome, especially when the race is going uphill.

The climbs took a toll on the peloton. It fractured into numerous groups on the first climb. The groups behind the leaders were only concerned about making the time cut, which is a percentage of the winner's time. The *gruppettos* were full of the sprinters, the *domestiques*, and the riders who were sick or too tired to push on in the front.

The *gruppettos* got bigger each day and in the final week they seemed to be larger than the lead peloton. Everybody felt the effects of the heat and the altitude in the mountains for the last week. I was in a group with Dave Zabriskie. We didn't talk much in the group; we all simply focused on the wheel in front of us and getting to the line. The Italians found enough energy to whistle and yell at the girls who cheered us on from the roadside, and everybody in the group took a quick glance.

Finally, the finish line appeared in front of us. Beyond the line we saw Elvio and Richard, two of our *soigneurs*, pointing us toward the bus and holding out some fresh drinks. The two of them are also ready

DOMESTIQUE: *Ekimov retrieves water bottles for his teammates.*

with clean clothes and towels, in case we need to go to the podium or to a random doping control as stage winners. The bus is a few hundred meters beyond the line. I passed my bike off to Geoff Brown, the mechanic, and climbed aboard the bus. Geoff, a fellow Canadian, has worked alongside Lance since his days on Motorola in the early 1990s. The mechanics take a lot of pride in their jobs and they are a crucial link in the chain that makes the team.

Towels and wash lotion were ready and sitting next to our bags so that we could get cleaned up. After four hours in the saddle, we are covered in salt, sticky energy drink, and road dirt—a wipe down feels really good and a shower at the hotel feels even better. A bag of sandwiches, tuna salad on a baguette, was passed around the bus along with drinks as we leaned back on the couches and talked about the race.

My cell phone rang, and it was Dede, who had just finished watching the race on TV in Girona. I asked her what happened in the final hour of the race, because the only knowledge I had of what happened in front of me was from what Johan said over the radio, as he encouraged Triki and Floyd up front. We spoke about the race, her day, what she was doing for dinner tonight. After a bit, I told her I'd call her back when I got settled in the hotel.

When the bus rolled up to the hotel, Alejandro was waiting at the reception area with our room keys. The suitcases were already in our rooms. The first thing I did was get into the shower; the hot water helped my ears and my congested nose to drain.

In Alejandro's room, there were snacks: potatoes that Willy had boiled up for us, cereals, drinks, fruit, and cookies. I ate a few potatoes with olive oil and salt and had a yogurt drink. I walked back to my room to check my e-mail and talk with Dede a bit longer.

An hour later, Alejandro came by my room to get me for a massage. Each rider spends about 45 minutes on the massage table each night, getting the knots worked out of his legs and his back muscles relaxed. We listened to Leonard Cohen as he massaged my sore legs and back. My pelvis and hip were feeling better although I still felt sharp pains when I accelerated hard in the saddle. The bone on my backside was still sensitive, and when Jandro's hands passed over the spot every muscle in my body contracted to protect it.

For a few hours between two stages, I could escape. It felt good to be done with a stage, with the effort, and to relax without having to think too much about the next day's race. The music helped take me away. My thoughts wandered to home, to friends, to family, to sleep.

Forty-five minutes had passed and I climbed off the massage table, my legs and back refreshed and greasy from the massage cream. I left the cream on my legs and hoped its arnica would speed my muscle recovery. I pulled on my tension socks, and then my sweatpants over that, and walked to the elevator that would take me to dinner. Even when there is only one flight with a dozen or so stairs to the lobby, after a race day cyclists wait for the elevator. Stairs are not an option.

Dinner was served at 9 p.m. At the dinner table there were white bread rolls at each place setting, a couple of bottles of mineral water, sparkling and flat, and two bowls of salad. Each night in each hotel, the setting is the same. The salad consists of tuna, corn, tomatoes, white asparagus, and iceberg lettuce. We had been eating the same salad since the start of the Vuelta and it would most likely take us to the finish. Few of us even ate it anymore.

MAX WAS APPALLED THAT THE STAFF WOULD EAT ICE CREAM IN FRONT OF US AND SAID THAT IT WAS RUDE AND UNFAIR. BUT SINCE WE NEED TO PEDAL UP HILLS, LET THEM EAT THEIR ICE CREAM AND FRIES.

Strangely, in each hotel, the waiter also brought a separate bowl of pale, canned, shredded carrots soaked in vinegar; these were never touched. We ate the bread first, dipping it in olive oil with salt or Parmesan cheese while we waited for Willy to come out with our pasta. His dishes are always the center of the meal; most of us just ate his pasta or rice dishes and skipped the rest of the meal cooked by the hotel staff. We would also eat a piece of meat, more out of necessity than desire.

The race results are brought to the table by a courier dressed in yellow motorcycle gear with the race sponsors' logos covering each sleeve and pant leg. Johan hands over a copy and keeps another one to look over.

The staff sits at a separate table from the riders. Each team uses the same layout. The riders often eat at different times than the staff and also have different menus. The staff will eat steak and fries with ice cream for dessert, while we eat pasta, salad, and steak with yogurt for dessert. Max was appalled that the staff would eat ice cream in front of us and said that it was rude and unfair. But since we need to pedal up hills, let them eat their ice cream and fries.

The conversation at dinner often revolves around the day's race. My mind was in a fog from my cold, and I felt as though I was underwater. After getting our yogurt, we piled into the elevator and went back to our rooms, making a stop at Jandro's room for cookies.

I got online one more time, checked out the news, and answered a few e-mails. I escaped for a few minutes by reading the news from Boulder and Toronto, what my friends were up to, how their jobs were going, and what the weather was like. Toronto was changing colors; fall was in the air and the guys on the local club ride, the "donut ride," were already wearing their leg warmers and long-sleeve jerseys. Here in Spain, I had just raced with my jersey wide open, covered in sweaty salt at the end of the day, and could only fall asleep if the air conditioner was on. I thought back to high school, riding back and forth on my bike, my first girlfriend, cross-country running, raking leaves, and drinking tea on the back porch with my dad.

Jandro knocked on the door. I opened the door and he handed me my laundry bag, filled with my clean race clothes. I threw the bag in my backpack, which I'd take to the race the next day, and continued reading my e-mail.

It is hard to fall asleep after racing in the late afternoon and then eating after 9 o'clock. I lay in bed, my computer on my lap, and watched an episode of the BBC sitcom *The Office* that my buddy had sent me on DVD to keep me entertained through the race. Each night I watched an episode or two before sleep.

The phone rang, and it was my friend Joe from Toronto. Joe and I grew up together in the city, went to the same kindergarten, and then raced together as teenagers. We spoke for an hour. It was 11:30 when his calling card ran out—time for bed.

The first big training loops I did as a 14-year-old were with Joe. We both had fixed-gear bikes for the winter months, cyclo-cross bikes for the fall, and racing bikes for the summer. At the end of my street was a mirrored-glass office tower, in which we would check out our style and our positions on the bike, making sure we looked like pros, imitating Laurent Fignon, Sean Kelly, and Gert-Jan Theunisse. We occasionally got lost on our bikes in the heart of the city, stranded in the pouring rain or driving snow, our wool jerseys smelling like a wet cat and no money in our pockets to get home. I would call home for a ride when it was snowing and I was north of the city, eating pastries in an Italian bakery, and my mom would tell me I'd better get myself home, that she wasn't driving 60 kilometers (37 miles) to pick me up. My mom went back on this threat and rescued us once when it was sleeting and too dark to ride, but on the other occasions we always made it home, fueled by cookies from the corner store, knowing it would make us tough. Anyway, the real pros in Europe would be out riding in the bad weather and so we should be, too.

Joe drank fifteen cups of tea one evening trying to get warm after our ride. With each cup he dipped a jam-filled cookie in his tea.

After dinner, when Joe slept over, we would sit up in the bedroom, listening to Pink Floyd and Led Zeppelin on my record player. "Houses of the Holy" and "The Wall" now bring back memories of riding in the parks on our 'cross bikes, covered in fall mud, thinking about nothing but cycling and girls. I don't think either of us did much homework in high school.

My house became a center for cycling. Each evening after school, we would meet at the house, eat a few butter tarts, ride until dark, and then come back, put on records, and talk around the dining room table with cups of tea.

When it was too cold to ride, we would play pick-up hockey at the local rink. Two blocks from the rink you could hear the game being played, the puck hitting the boards, guys yelling for passes and cheering when the goal was scored. To get around town, to the rink, to school, we rode our bikes, even when the weather kept most people off the streets. The sticks were strapped to the top frame tube with leather straps. The skates and gloves were carried in school backpacks. We played for hours, until it was dark, not thinking about our worried moms or dinner or homework, just thinking about the next goal. Then it was the next goal to win, until finally the rink closed and we had to go home. On the way home, we inhaled slices of pizza and Cokes. Then we were back to cruising on our city bikes, our "treaders," as we called them, with snow spraying up from the tires and cars honking at us to get off the road.

As kids riding in the parks or north of the city, we had been fueled by thoughts of one day being in the pro peloton, racing up the mountains in Europe. After getting off the phone with Joe, I rested, trying to fall asleep but also thinking about the next day, which would involve more mountains, a bit of crosswind, and intense heat.

CHAPTER NINETEEN

SEASON'S END

At the start of the Vuelta, we had sat down as a team and talked about our goals for the race. The team time trial was our first goal. From there we would aim for stage victories, first in the field sprints with Max and second as individuals trying to win out of breakaways. Max mentioned that the third and eleventh stages were the ones he was looking to win. But the third stage ended up being too difficult an uphill sprint for him, and he didn't make it to the eleventh stage. Dave Zabriskie made it to the eleventh stage and rode away with the victory.

Dave's attack had been subdued—he simply rolled off the front of the field a few kilometers faster than the rest of us and never looked back. It wasn't planned and certainly wasn't textbook. Many of the teams in the peloton were confused by the tactic, as we once again were in a position where we didn't have to chase and defend the jersey, or do an ounce of work in the wind. Perhaps offense was the best defense.

Alejandro Valverde, one of the favorites for the overall victory, broke his chain in mid-acceleration and crashed heavily, allowing Dave's breakaway to build up an even more solid lead. The field came to a near halt as we waited until Valverde was comfortably back in the saddle. In cycling it is an unwritten rule that when there is a bad crash or a favorite for the race victory crashes, the peloton slows down and waits until the riders are back in the peloton and all right.

Dave did an incredible job holding off the peloton. Rarely does a solo escape starting from the first kilometer stay away until the finish, because the sprinters' teams get to the front and collaborate on ensuring a field sprint. The teams began their pursuit of Dave, but he stayed focused and fast, averaging 40 kilometers per hour (25 mph) for four hours straight. In the final kilometers, he had begun to crack—physically and mentally—but he pushed through to hold off the peloton by just over 1 minute.

As we went through the small towns along the course, the crowds in the south of Spain were much larger than when we were farther north. There are not nearly as many roads in Spain as in France, so we end up racing along many highways through arid, empty countryside.

Soon after stage 11 was over, we showered in the bus and got ready for a two-hour transfer to Almería. Sandwiches were handed out; we got settled in our spots on the bus and rested.

In Almería, we moved into a nice beachside hotel for the first rest day and slept in for the first time in weeks. The next day, we had a late breakfast and then went for a couple hours' ride on the bikes.

The countryside in Almería is blanketed in plastic-covered greenhouses. From a distance they look like water or a lake, but up close they look basically like houses covered in plastic bags. Most of the fruit and vegetables for Europe are produced in the greenhouse-farming region in Almería.

The rest day had been eagerly awaited by all of us. More than a physical rest, we could enjoy a mental rest from the stress of the race.

GRAHAM WATSON

CAPTAIN COURAGEOUS: *David Zabriskie is relieved after a daring 160-km solo breakaway.*

On paper, the stage to the Observatorio Meteorológico de Calar Alto would be the hardest of the race, with three Category-1 climbs that would take us from the hot desert around Almería up into the humid clouds at the top of the mountain.

From the start the stage was fast, with attacks keeping the pace intense until the moment we hit the bottom of the first climb, an hour into the race. Liberty Seguros, Roberto Heras's team, had taken control of the race from the first few kilometers; Roberto was the best climber in the race and his team was racing to put him in the leader's jersey at day's end. Without a doubt this stage suited a pure climber like Roberto perfectly, since it was essentially all uphill or downhill from start to finish. At the base of the first climb the group splintered, and small groups of riders became scattered up the mountainside. The *gruppetto* was immediately at 60 or so riders. Once everybody was together and settled down, it would become the largest compact group riding to the finish. Ahead of the *gruppetto* the race fractured several times on the long mountain slopes.

Since the stage was short, 145 kilometers (90 miles) with a lot of climbing, it would be a challenge for the dropped riders in the *gruppetto* to make the time cut. At the end of the day, the group of 80 did not make the time cut and was over the limit by about 3 minutes. It was important for the group to stay together so that nobody would be eliminated—the *commissaires* cannot pull 80 riders from the race for missing the time cut, but they can pull smaller groups or individuals.

I was happy to find my spot in the *gruppetto* at the bottom of the climb, since I had been having such a rough time kicking my cold. The Italians, being the most vocal, tend to dictate the speed at which we ride. Going down the mountains we went at breakneck speeds, while going up we simply rode a steady rhythm that would keep the group together but still get us to the line in reasonable time.

Fortunately, many of the roads we raced on in the Vuelta had been repaved a few months before the race. It is much easier to race up and down mountain roads on smooth blacktop. Matt White had tried to ride on some of the climbs around his home in Valencia a month before the Vuelta. They were impassable gravel roads with potholes, but by the time we were racing they were as smooth as a speedway.

Floyd, Triki, and Victor raced up front in the lead group that was being pulled by a motivated Liberty Seguros. Interestingly, that team had consistently put riders in the breakaways, then they chased them down from behind. It was not the best tactic and we couldn't figure out why they were doing it, since they were burning up a lot of energy and ended up doing the work for their competitors. At the end of the day, Floyd lost the yellow jersey. But both Floyd and Triki held tough in the final climb, and retained their positions in the top 10 overall.

Sandwiched between two tough mountain stages, there was a flat stage along the southern coastline of Spain. It turned out to be a nice day of recovery for most of the peloton. It was the sprinters' last opportunity to vie for a stage victory.

From the start of the stage it was clear the Fassa Bortolo team was going to control the race from start to finish so that Petacchi could get a clean run at his fourth stage victory.

The course was undulating as we raced along highways, following the contours of the coastline. Halfway through the stage, the greenhouses of Almería were replaced by green hills covered with trees and vegetation. Triki lives fairly close to this area and pointed out the avocado and fruit trees, and the typical white houses (whole towns are white). The area is called Costa Tropical.

It was a fairly uneventful stage—we soaked up the sun, sat on the wheels, and watched the kilometers tick by as Fassa Bortolo kept the pace high and steady on the front of the group.

After we left the coast in the south, the remaining stages were for the pure climbers, with one hard day in the mountains followed by a long 30-kilometer (18.5-mile) uphill time trial. On both days,

Santiago Perez of the Phonak team dominated the stages, winning with ease and boosting him into third place overall behind Roberto Heras and Alejandro Valverde.

We were two weeks into the two-week race, and everybody on the team was getting a bit homesick. We had been together for nearly three weeks straight, since we arrived at the start in León three days before the race began, and we were ready for a change of pace, a change in diet, and a change in schedule. The team's morale was still good but we were looking toward the end. The consensus was pretty much that three weeks of anything with all the same people, even sitting on the beach, might just be a bit too much.

> THERE WAS A SECTION OF BEER-FUELED SPANIARDS THAT HAD FORMED TWO LINES ON EITHER SIDE OF THE ROAD AND YELLED "OLÉ" WHILE WAVING THEIR HATS LIKE TOREADORS AS WE RACED BY.

In the uphill time trial to the ski station of Sierra Nevada most of the team took it easy and went just hard enough to ensure they would make the time cut. Triki and Floyd obviously had to give it an all-out effort to hold on to their top 10 placement, but the rest of us had nothing to gain and a lot of energy to lose by riding as hard as possible.

The first section of the climb was a steep ascent out of Monachil, a small town on the outskirts of Grenada. The road twists up the mountainside for 5 kilometers, at very steep grades, before dropping down for a few kilometers and joining up with the shallower climb up to the Sierra Nevada ski station. The 30 kilometers (18.5 miles) of roadside were peppered with spectators. It was nice to have encouragement, and a little distraction from the effort, as we were climbing the hill. There was a section of beer-fueled Spaniards that had formed two lines on either side of the road and yelled "*olé*" while waving their hats like toreadors as we raced by. I noticed penises painted on the climbs, similar to those painted on the Tour roads, so I wondered if the same crew made their way from the Alps down to southern Spain to decorate the mountain roads. And why?

In the evening after the time trial to the top of the Sierra Nevada, the entire Vuelta—the peloton, the directors, the *commissaires*, and the organizers—piled onto two airplanes for a flight from Grenada to Badajoz. There, buses were lined up to take us to the hotels in Olivenza.

As we headed into the last week of racing, Roberto Heras was holding a slim lead over Alejandro Valverde. The race had left the southern coast. We would be heading into the region where Roberto lives and riding through the mountains he grew up climbing. His motivation would be high.

The second rest day was mellow—an easy ride through the countryside followed by a few kilometers of motorpacing behind the team car to open our legs up for the stages to come. The countryside on the midwestern side of Spain is much like the terrain around Santa Barbara, California, with cattle in the fields between hillsides covered in olive groves. The area is well known for the Spanish delicacy Iberic ham. While riding we saw a few sties full of *pata negra* pigs, which have black feet and are fed acorns to give the cured ham a nutty flavor. A good guy or a nice person in Spanish slang is called a *pata negra*, and calling someone this is a true compliment.

The morning after the rest day we were all back down at breakfast ready to eat for the day's stage. As we sat at the breakfast table Dede called to wish me a good morning and good luck for the race, and then she added that she had read on the Internet that Tyler Hamilton had tested positive for blood doping. At the breakfast table we went silent in disbelief. Within hours the news had spread through the hotel, and at the start, it was all the riders and media were talking about. But soon enough the starter's pistol was fired and the race started out of the blocks with attacks being launched up and down the rolling hills that cut through the olive groves surrounding Olivenza.

The course toward Madrid was in the wide-open outback of Spain, with dry prairie and olive trees scattered over the countryside. The sun beat down on us relentlessly. Within hours salt was covering everybody. Riders were constantly going back to their team cars for bottles. Within about 15 minutes the water was as warm as bathwater and had a plastic taste to it. The thermometer in the car read 39 to 40 degrees Celsius throughout the day (104°F).

We started stage 17 on a climb, in the baking sun. Immediately I could see that more than half of the peloton was uncomfortable. The race had been hard for 10 days and many riders were sick. Once we hit the second climb of the day and the pace increased, *gruppettos* were quickly formed. The majority of the peloton left the climbers up ahead to battle for the victory and the race lead.

Antonio, Victor, Dave, and I quickly found our spot in the *gruppetto* and settled in for the ride. Nobody in the group of 30 riders spoke much as everyone was beaten down and tired out. The key to riding in the *gruppetto* is to take it as easy as possible and still make it within the time cut. At the same time, the Italians go like crazy on the descents and are constantly running up other riders' backsides, as if they were stuck in Milan traffic on a Friday afternoon. At the end of a long day with many climbs in the intense sunshine and heat, small things can become annoying.

Stage 17 was in the heart of Roberto Heras territory. His name was painted about a thousand times on the course. Roberto was born in the town where we stayed after the stage, Bejar. The town is shadowed by the mountain we had just climbed. Laudelino Cubino, a famous Spanish cyclist from the previous decade, owns the hotel where we stayed. The lobby was covered in pictures from his days in the peloton.

Floyd and Victor both got sick and Dave suffered from heatstroke during the stage and didn't make it to the line. Dave had to get off and sit down until he found a ride in the team car and while he was sitting there some spectators rode his bike up and down the road until he finally yelled at them to leave it alone. It was not a great day for the team.

The last couple of days of the race only got worse: Floyd stopped due to the same cold that had caused me to stop the previous day. We were close to the end but the team that had started the race as one of the strongest had come to pieces with five days to go.

Despite the fact that Postal finished with a skeleton crew of riders and staff, the Vuelta was a successful race for us. We accomplished the majority of our goals with stage victories, many riders sharing the leader's jersey, and several riders taking top places in stages. Triki finished well overall, and Floyd would most likely have held on to finish in the top 10 had he not become sick in the final week of the race. For most of the team the season was over, and it would be their last trip on the U.S. Postal bus.

The U.S. Postal team bus made its final trip around

Europe during the 2004 season. No longer will the eagle fly through the Alps, over the cobbles of the Arenberg Forest, or down the Champs-Elysées.

I finished the season at the world championships in Verona, Italy. The same week Dave Zabriskie raced his last race on a Trek bike in the time trial at the world championships, doing a terrific ride to finish in fifth place. Verona was Dede's last race and she retired after she crossed the line.

I left Verona with mixed emotions. I was happy to be done with the season and able to rest my legs while enjoying time at home with Dede, but I was also disappointed as I crashed out of the race three-quarters of the way through. I was left wondering "What if?" because I had been feeling fantastic prior to crashing.

I was happy to see Dede cross the line with a smile on her face knowing it would be her last race. She rode the race with the same enthusiastic effort she has given throughout her career as a cyclist. Dede has had an incredible career with victories or podium finishes in virtually every race on the women's calendar and she was able to complete her dream by winning a medal at the Olympics. She is content with her career as a bike racer but she will always be a cyclist, as she loves to ride. There is simply too much else in life she wants to discover away from the cycling world.

CASEY B GIBSON

NEW LINE UP: *Damon Kluck finishes his cycling career with the '04 season.*

Over the winter, the team vehicles would be stripped down and redressed with the globe logo of the Discovery Channel. The old team bus would be relegated to the smaller races and replaced by a new, larger bus to accommodate the expanded team of riders and staff.

The team would have a new look in 2005 with Discovery Channel as the title sponsor, but the same core group of riders and staff, built around Lance, should ensure that the foundation of the organization remains the same. Gone are Floyd Landis, Victor Hugo Peña, and Dave Zabriskie, who have joined other European squads where they will pursue different goals in a new environment. *Soigneurs* Freddy Viaene and Alejandro Vasquez will be missed as well, for their organizational skills, their welcome at the airport, and their quality massages. Damon Kluck has retired from racing and his mellow demeanor and dry sense of humor will be irreplaceable. Daniel Rincon has moved on as well, and I will always remember his permanent smile that was evident even when we were racing in pouring rain. Robbie Ventura and Kenny Labbe, the

U.S.–based riders on the team, have also retired after being fixtures on the American race scene since the 1980s.

There would be new faces integrated into the team, making it not only larger but also more diverse. But in a few months, all the riders would be united under one jersey with the same goals. The Discovery Channel team added Giro d'Italia champion Paolo Salvodelli to its roster as well as Yaroslav Popovych, a talented young

CASEY B. GIBSON

RETIRED: *Robbie Ventura pulls out of a corner at the New York City Championships.*

grand tour rider, and the classics team was bolstered with Roger Hammond and Leif Hoste, two of the riders who animated the cobbled classics in 2004.

The U.S. Postal team has written history in cycling. The team has gone from a small U.S. squad with a goal to enter the Tour de France to six-time Tour champions who inspired millions of people around the world, drawing noncycling fans to learn about the sport of cycling and to dream in yellow.

I look forward to the coming seasons, racing throughout the world with a group of friends who are passionate about pedaling.

Michael Barry grew up immersed in Toronto's cycling culture, due in large part to his father, a former bicycle racer from Wimbledon, England. Mike Barry Sr. immigrated to Toronto, Canada and opened a bike shop in 1972.

Michael spent his childhood pedaling around the city, racing through the parks, dreaming of one day following in the footsteps of his favorite European professional cyclists. While attending high school at Upper Canada College, he was recruited by the Canadian national team, and his international cycling career began. A pivotal year in his development as a cyclist was 1996, when Michael went to France to race with an amateur team, Velo Club Annemasse. Upon gaining experience and strength in the European peloton, he earned himself a spot on the 1996 Canadian Olympic Team and rode in support of one of his mentors and childhood heroes, Steve Bauer. Two years later, Michael signed his first professional contract with the North America–based Saturn cycling team. He made rapid progress there, and in 2001 he was given the chance to race alongside Lance Armstrong on the U.S. Postal team, arguably the number one team in the world.

Michael's experiences on U.S. Postal have challenged him professionally and culturally as he has had the incredible opportunity to travel and work with teammates from around the world.

Michael and his wife, Olympian Dede Demet Barry, split their time between Boulder, Colorado and Girona, Spain.